TEENS & the Media

ROGER E. HERNÁNDEZ

THE GALLUP YOUTH SURVEY:
MAJOR ISSUES AND TRENDS

TEENS & the Media

ROGER E. HERNÁNDEZ

Produced by OTTN Publishing, Stockton, New Jersey

Mason Crest Publishers
370 Reed Road
Broomall, PA 19008
www.masoncrest.com

First printing

1 3 5 7 9 8 6 4 2

Library of Congress Cataloging-in-Publication Data

Hernández, Roger E.
  Teens and the media / Roger E. Hernandez.
      p. cm. — (The Gallup Youth Survey, major issues and trends)
  Includes bibliographical references and index.
  ISBN 1-59084-874-8
  1. Mass media and teenagers. 2. Mass media and teenagers—United
States. I. Title. II. Series.
  HQ799.2.M35.H48 2004
  302.23'0835—dc22
                          2004022607

Contents

Introduction

By George Gallup

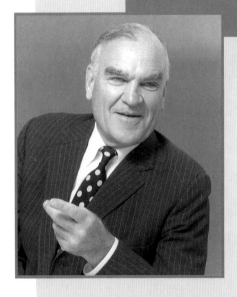

As the United States moves into the new century, there is a vital need for insight into what it means to be a young person in America. Today's teenagers—the so-called "Y Generation"—will be the leaders and shapers of the 21st century. The future direction of the United States is being determined now in their hearts and minds and actions. Yet how much do we as a society know about this important segment of the U.S. populace who have the potential to lift our nation to new levels of achievement and social health?

The nation's teen population will top 30 million by the year 2006, the highest number since 1975. Most of these teens will grow up to be responsible citizens and leaders. But some youths face very long odds against reaching adulthood physically safe, behaviorally sound, and economically self-supporting. The challenges presented to society by the less fortunate youth are enormous. To help meet these challenges it is essential to have an accurate picture of the present status of teenagers.

The Gallup Youth Survey—the oldest continuing survey of teenagers—exists to help society meet its responsibility to youth, as well as to inform and guide our leaders by probing the social and economic attitudes and behaviors of young people. With theories abounding about the views, lifestyles, and values of adolescents, the Gallup Youth Survey, through regular scientific measurements of teens themselves, serves as a sort of reality check.

We need to hear more clearly the voices of young people, and to help them better articulate their fears and their hopes. Our youth have much to share with their elders—is the older generation really listening? Is it carefully monitoring the hopes and fears of teenagers today? Failure to do so could result in severe social consequences.

Surveys reveal that the image of teens in the United States today is a negative one. Teens are frequently maligned, misunderstood, or simply ignored by their elders. Yet two decades of the Gallup Youth Survey have provided ample evidence of the very special qualities of the nation's youngsters. In fact, if our society is less racist, less sexist, less polluted, and more peace loving, we can in considerable measure thank our young people, who have been on the leading edge on these issues.

And the younger generation is not geared to greed: survey after survey has shown that teens have a keen interest in helping those people, especially in their own communities, who are less fortunate than themselves

Young people tell the Gallup Youth Survey that they are enthusiastic about helping others, and are willing to work for world peace and a healthy world. They feel positive about their schools and even more positive about their teachers. A large majority of American teenagers report that they are happy and excited about the future, feel very close to their families, are likely to marry, want to have children, are satisfied with their personal lives, and desire to reach the top of their chosen careers.

But young adults face many threats, so parents, guardians, and concerned adults must commit themselves to do everything possible to help tomorrow's parents, citizens, and leaders avoid or overcome risky behaviors so that they can move into the future with greater hope and understanding.

The Gallup Organization and the Gallup Youth Survey are enthusiastic about this partnership with Mason Crest Publishers. Through carefully and clearly written books on a variety of vital topics dealing with teens, Gallup Youth Survey statistics are presented in a way that gives new depth and meaning to the data. The focus of these books is a practical one—to provide readers with the statistics and solid information that they need to understand and to deal with each important topic.

* * *

Readers will find *Teens and the Media* to be a fascinating historical account of the interaction between the teenage population and the media in all its forms, since the beginning of the youth culture in the 1950s when the word "teenager" first came into use.

The author draws upon pertinent data from surveys and other sources in examining the impact, both positive and negative, of the media on young lives, and how it shapes their likes and dislikes. Quotes from survey respondents illustrate the statistics.

Looking ahead, Hernández speculates about the growing reach and influence of the Internet and predict that "media convergence"—all mass media coming together through the computer—is the wave of the future.

Chapter One

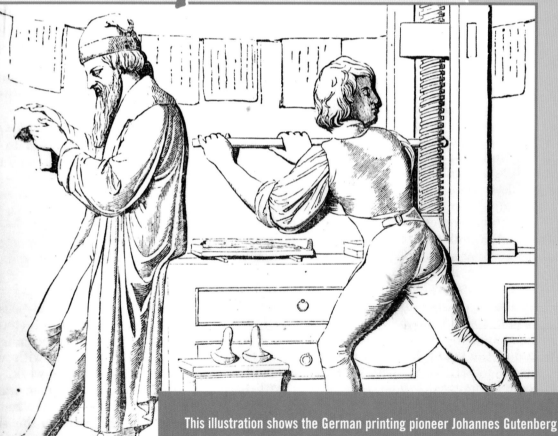

This illustration shows the German printing pioneer Johannes Gutenberg checking his work while his assistant turns the press. The development of the printing press in the 15th century led to widespread distribution of published materials such as books, newspapers, and pamphlets.

Teenagers and the Mass Media

"During their waking hours, teens live in a world of music and sound," says George Gallup, Jr., chairman of the George H. Gallup International Institute. "On the radio, through Walkmans or boom boxes, music videos on TV, and in other ways." In other words, the lives of teenagers are immersed in what is produced by the media. This is not just an American phenomenon—the mass media have become so pervasive that young people from Brazil to Norway to Japan watch their local versions of MTV, go online, listen to music on the radio, and read publications about their favorite singers, actors and sports stars.

But what, exactly, is meant by "media?" The word *media* is the plural of "medium," which the Merriam-Webster online dictionary defines as "a channel or system of communication, information, or entertainment." More specifically, the *mass media* refers to means of communication designed to reach a large number of people. Mass media are a relatively new phenomenon in the history of humankind. And only in the past few decades have the media begun to shape the likes and dislikes of teenagers.

Early Days of the Media

The beginnings of mass media can be traced to the middle of the 15th century. Before then, books or pamphlets were written by hand—each individual copy had to be made one page at a time, one letter at a time. It took months or even years to make a single book, so it was not practical to make a lot of copies. Besides, most people did not know how to read. So very few books or pamphlets were published, very few copies were made of each publication, and very few people ever read them.

This began to change after Johannes Gutenberg invented a printing press that used movable type—blocks made of lead, with individual letters and punctuation symbols raised above the surface on one side of the block. Letters could be arranged together to form the text of an entire page, stained with ink, and finally impressed against a piece of paper by Gutenberg's printing press. The process could be repeated many times, producing multiple copies of the same page. Then the blocks of letters could be rearranged to form the words for the next page, those pages would be also be printed, and so on. At the end the pages were put in order, bound together—and the result was a book, or books, made in a fraction of the time it would have taken with handwriting. In the 1450s Gutenberg printed a Bible, the first time a book was published in large numbers.

At first only books or the occasional pamphlets were printed, but by the end of that century news sheets—an early version of newspapers—began to circulate in some German cities. By the 1700s, as literacy grew, regularly scheduled newspapers began to appear in Europe and North America. A century later newspapers, along with the first regularly scheduled magazines, had become truly mass media, disseminating news and information to millions of readers eager to know what was going on in their hometowns or on the far side of the globe, and also influencing decision makers.

Today, teens have access to a variety of electronic media that was not available a century ago, including radio, television, and the Internet.

Print media reigned unchallenged until broadcast media came along. Radio was first, establishing its popularity in the 1920s. Families would gather around large radio sets in the living room and listen to music or hear, live, the actual voices of people in the news. Then in the 1950s television came along, adding visuals to the mix and providing unforgettable moving images that neither radio or print media could match. Over the next years television became a dominant medium for teen audiences. They had not been born during the days radio or print were most popular, so they did not know a world without TV.

By the early 1990s it seemed that the world of mass media was set. There was print, which included newspapers and magazines. And there was broadcast, which included radio and television. But then a revolutionary new medium, the Internet, came into widespread use. The Internet combined features of other media. A user could read an article as in a printed publication, listen to music like on the radio, or watch video like on television. The Internet also brought features other media do not offer, such as interactivity and a global reach.

Teens in particular were quick to jump on the Internet. A Japanese teenager is now a click away from listening to rap music; an American teenager is now a click away from reading a Japanese *manga* comic book. Many teens have also set up their own websites. Theoretically, anyone anywhere in the world with an Internet connection can visit those sites, making their webmasters part of the mass media too in a way.

The Media and Teenagers

Despite the growing importance of the internet, the mass media with the most influence and largest audiences continue to be long-established publications, big-time *broadcast networks,* and the websites owned by large companies. How much attention do these powerful media institutions pay to teenagers? It depends. Newspapers and most television networks, for instance, still cater mostly to adults. Yet there are *cable networks*, radio stations, and magazines that aim specifically at teenagers. Their very survival depends on attracting teen viewers, teen listeners, and teen readers.

This youth-oriented media is a fairly new phenomenon. Teens today take it for granted that they can watch a teen-oriented drama series on a network television station, then switch over to MTV to catch a music video. But a generation ago a few radio stations and a handful of magazines were the only media that catered to teens. Today, mass media executives recognize teenagers as a distinctive group in American life with lots of spending power. Advertisers are eager to reach that audience, which encouraged major media companies over the last two decades to launch new publications and television programs aimed squarely at young people.

Teens have been just as eager to watch, listen, or read. Today, so many teens use media and so many media outlets are reaching out to teens that their relationship has become a two-way street. Young people are deeply influenced by the content provided by the mass media, at the same time that the mass media is becoming deeply influenced by what teens want.

Chapter Two

A generation ago national television news was dominated by the three major broadcast networks, so the stories that news anchors like Walter Cronkite chose to report gained the most attention. Today, the networks have become less important as a variety of other television news sources are available for adult and teen viewers.

Television's Growing Focus on Teens

On December 9, 1980, a newly formed labor union in Poland was challenging the ruling Communist regime and taking on the Cold War power of the Soviet Union. American hostages passed their 13th month of captivity by Islamic radicals who had taken over the U.S. embassy in Tehran, Iran. And in Washington, D.C., Ronald Reagan was preparing to succeed Jimmy Carter as president of the United States. Yet at 7 P.M. that night television viewers across the nation heard Walter Cronkite, the most traditional of news anchors, begin the CBS Evening News by saying, "The death of a man who sang and played guitar overshadows the news from Poland, Iran, and Washington tonight."

The singer and guitar player Cronkite referred to was John Lennon, a former member of the rock group the Beatles, who had been shot to death outside his New York apartment. But the *lead* for the program indicated that Cronkite felt he had to explain to his mostly adult viewers that those in charge of the news program had deliberately decided that the death of a teen idol deserved to be the top story that day instead of other, more conventional stories about politics and world affairs. It was a signal that something was changing in American television.

The old generation that had controlled the medium since its inception in the 1950s never paid much attention to young people. Public television has long had shows for children such as *Sesame Street*, but even today PBS offers little specifically for teens. Some television programs in the 1960s and 1970s featured teenage characters, such as *The Many Loves of Dobie Gillis, My Three Sons, Leave it to Beaver*, and *The Partridge Family*, but the target audience for these shows was families, rather than just teen viewers. Commercial stations carried Dick Clark's Saturday afternoon *American Bandstand*, and rock groups appeared on such popular family programs as *The Ed Sullivan Show* or *The Smothers Brothers Comedy Hour*. In the 1970s shows like *The Midnight Special* broadcast rock concerts in the late evenings. Beyond that, there was little programming solely for teens.

However, by the early 1980s media executives began to understand the rising power of youth culture—that things which interested young people were important, and that some of them were **newsworthy** enough to merit prominent national coverage.

Today teenagers are no longer an afterthought on television—they are a sought-after **demographic**. Tweens and young teens have entire cable networks devoted to them, such as Nickelodeon's The N and the Disney Channel. Older teens have MTV on cable plus the dozens of youth-oriented shows that broadcast networks Fox, WB, and UPN have presented since the early 1990s.

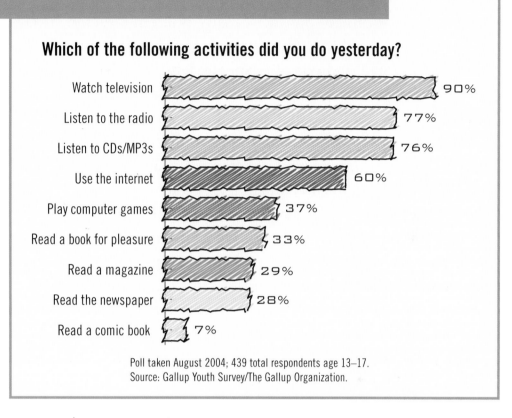

Which of the following activities did you do yesterday?

Activity	Percentage
Watch television	90%
Listen to the radio	77%
Listen to CDs/MP3s	76%
Use the internet	60%
Play computer games	37%
Read a book for pleasure	33%
Read a magazine	29%
Read the newspaper	28%
Read a comic book	7%

Poll taken August 2004; 439 total respondents age 13–17.
Source: Gallup Youth Survey/The Gallup Organization.

What caused this change is the coming together of three factors. One is that a members of a different age group now run the television industry. Many producers and executives are members of the "Baby Boom" generation, a nickname given to people born between 1946 and 1964. The Baby Boomers were the first generation for which a distinctive youth culture emerged. Members of that generation recognized the power of marketing to teens, and they moved toward more youth-oriented programming. Another factor is the rising affluence of teens. Americans from 13 to 19 years old spend nearly $100 billion for goods and services annually, according to 12 to 20, a marketing firm that specializes in young people. As a 2004 Gallup report recognized, "Television brought the world into everyone's living room, and along with it, ads for all kinds of new products, many of them targeted specifically to teens." The third influential force was the coming of cable television and its hundreds of channels, which allowed programmers to target specific groups of viewers, such as teens.

There is no question that teens have taken to television. A Gallup Youth Survey poll taken in 2002 found that nine in 10 teens watch TV on a daily basis. Another Gallup survey, in 2003, attempted to determine how much television teens watch. It found that 32 percent of young people said they watch between one to five hours a week; 30 percent said five to 10 hours; 20 percent said 10 to 20 hours; and 11 percent said they are in front of their sets more than 20 a week. Only 5 percent said they watched less than an hour a week, and just one in one hundred American teens said they watched no television at all.

The same poll also found boys are more avid viewers than girls. Among those who watch only one to five hours a week there were more females than males, 37 percent to 27 percent. But among those who watched 10 to 20 hours there were more males (23 percent) than females (17 percent). Most of those who spent even more time watching TV were boys too—14 percent of them said they watched more than 20 hours, compared to just 8 percent of girls.

Still, the gender differences are less pronounced than the broad trend, which is that teenagers love to watch television. And with all that disposable income, no one ought be surprised that the entertainment industry caters to teens. An analysis by the Gallup Organization described teens as "among the most rabid consumers of television fare."

Hours per Week Spent Watching TV, by Gender

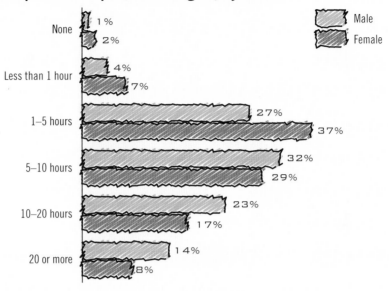

Hours per Week Spent Watching TV, by Age

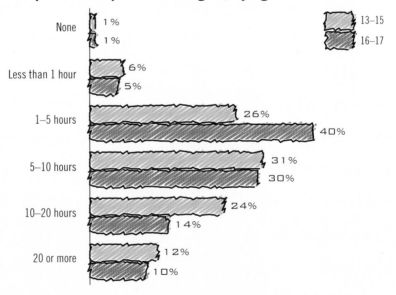

Poll taken August 2003; 517 total respondents age 13–17.
Source: Gallup Youth Survey/The Gallup Organization

However, not all of the television industry pays the same intense attention to teens. The traditional networks, their newer broadcast competitors, and cable stations all approach teen programming according to their own views of what is best for themselves.

The Mainstream Networks

The "Big Three" American television networks—ABC, CBS, and NBC—have been around almost as long as television itself. They first went on the air in an era when there were very few channel choices. In most cities throughout the country, the three television networks were the only options for those who wanted to watch national television news or programming. So the networks devoted themselves to programming primarily for adults, the widest audience available.

That tendency remains, because most Big Three shows continue to aim at an adult audience. Of course, teens also watch adult dramas like CBS's *CSI: Crime Scene Investigation*, or comedies such as NBC's *Friends*. According to Nielsen Media Research, a company that measures the viewership of television programs, the final episode of *Friends*, which aired during the May 2004 *sweeps*, was viewed by more than 52 million people. The show received a *rating* of 12.1 among viewers 15 to 20 years of age, meaning it was watched by 12.1 percent of all viewers in that age group. This made *Friends* the most-watched show among young people for the week. However, *Friends* is not specifically aimed at teenagers and does not have a predominantly teen audience. The episode's rating among all viewers was 29.8, significantly higher than its rating among young viewers.

Because of the networks' tendency to focus on adult programming, fewer teens are tuning in to the Big Three. By 2001, reported *Media Life* magazine, cable programming as a whole reached an 11.0 rating among teens, surpassing the 10.4 received by four major broadcast networks (this study included Fox with the older Big Three). "It's a widening gap and it's clearly about the programming," Joe Ostrow, then president and chief executive officer of the Cabletelevision Advertising Bureau, told the magazine.

Yet teens are not leaving all broadcast networks. They just seem to be tuning into networks other than the Big Three. The *Media Life* article noted that when two smaller and relatively young broadcast networks, WB and UPN, were included, the number of teens watching broadcast networks shot up to a 15.2 rating, easily surpassing cable. This can be attributed to the youth-oriented programming broadcast over these networks. The young audience enables them to compete with the Big Three for advertising dollars.

Young Networks for Young People

In 1986 the powerful media *conglomerate* News Corporation—owner of the movie studio Twentieth Century Fox as well as newspapers in the United States, Great Britain, and Australia—launched the fledgling Fox Network. Because the hold that ABC, CBS and NBC had on the adult audience seemed invulnerable at the time, Fox decided to bet on the young people that the Big Three was largely ignoring. It began to air programs with plenty of young stars and aimed them directly at a teenage audience. One of its first hits, *21 Jump Street,* was about youthful looking cops working undercover at a high school. It ran from 1987 to 1991 and starred Johnny Depp, who went on to become a movie star with a large teen following.

Fox did not just focus on young viewers; in the late 1980s and 1990s it attracted adults with such programs as *Married with Children* and *The X Files*, and both children and adults could enjoy the network's biggest hit, *The Simpsons*. Today, Fox programs like *American Idol* and *That '70s Show* are popular among teens but are not specifically aimed at teens. Yet youth remains important to Fox's overall ratings. In the May 2004 sweeps, for instance, nine of the 15 most popular shows among teens were on Fox compared to just three of 15 among adults—all of them episodes of *American Idol*. Fox also had the top-rated drama for teenagers, *The OC*, which did not make the top 50 among viewers of all ages.

Fox is not the only broadcast network looking to attract young people. Its initial success finding a teen audience caught the attention of executives at other large media companies, with the result that in the mid-1990s two new broadcast networks were born, WB and UPN. They knew, as the Gallup Youth Survey confirmed in 2002, that watching television was a teenage habit. Teens in that

Although a growing number of television shows are made for teen viewers, some media experts critcize the absence of major teen African American, Hispanic, or Asian characters on these programs.

poll ranked watching TV as their second-favorite way to spend an evening, after "visiting friends" and ahead of "spending time with family."

Critics say one problem with teen-oriented dramas is a lack of ethnic diversity. All of the main teen characters in the most popular shows of the mid-2000s—*The OC, One Tree Hill, Everwood*—are white. And when it comes to recurring adult characters only a handful are not white, such as Irv, the African American school bus driver in *Everwood*. One network that does feature young African Americans prominently is UPN, with programs such as *The Parkers, Eve,* and *Girlfriends*. Yet the target age group for many of its shows, the network says, is not the classic 13 to 18 teenage demographic but an older 18 to 34, with an emphasis on females. Besides, UPN couples its focus on young African-American women with a quite different emphasis on young males of any race, showing professional wrestling and action shows like *Star Trek: Enterprise*. Some critics have said the double-barreled approach keeps UPN from establishing a clear identity and capturing a larger audience.

UPN's competitor WB (owned by Time-Warner, a conglomerate that also runs several other big name media outlets, including HBO, CNN, the Warner Brothers movie studio, *Time* magazine, and AOL) has a stronger focus on teens overall. With teen series *Dawson's Creek, Buffy the Vampire Slayer,* and *Felicity* among its hits in the late 1990s, it sealed its image as the broadcast network devoted to viewers 13 to 18. The WB was the only broadcast network in a study by the Jack Myers Media Investors newsletter that teens ranked higher as "most entertaining" than adults, 51 to 49 percent.

With *One Tree Hill* and *Everwood,* WB continued to come up with programs for teenagers in the 2000s. It has not been shy, either, to inject teen sex into its shows hoping to increase ratings.

During the first week of the February 2004 sweeps, the plot of an *Everwood* episode had the main teenage character Ephram and his older girlfriend contemplating whether to sleep together. The drama continued the following week, when they did sleep together as an impressive teen viewership watched. It was the most popular WB show among teens for the week, according to *Media Life* magazine, and brought a record number of male teenagers to WB's Monday entire night lineup.

Too Spicy?

Everwood's ratings jump made executives at WB happy, but not everyone was as thrilled. Television in general, and teen-oriented shows in particular, have come under fire for raunchy language and increasingly graphic depictions of sex. A study by the Parents Television Council, a conservative media watchdog organization, said that "foul language" during the so-called Family Hour (8 to 9 P.M.) increased by 94.8 percent between 1998 and 2002, and by 109.1 percent in the time period that followed. In addition, said the study, "The teen-targeted WB network had a 188 percent increase in foul language during the Family Hour between 1998 and 2002. Such language increased by 308.5 percent during the second hour of prime time."

Overall, television is sending young people a mixed message about sex, says a 2004 study sponsored by Mediascope, another media watchdog group. "Explicit and implicit lessons ranged from 'Virginity is a sign that a boy is a loser' to 'Teens don't need to be sexually active to be cool,'" the report concluded. Does any of this have an effect on teen behavior? One study by the University of Michigan, cited by the PTC, concluded young women who watch as little as 22 hours a month of prime time TV tend to have more sex partners and "are more likely to endorse a 'recreational' view of sex than young women who watch less TV."

There is also the issue of homosexuality. Most teen dramas approach it sparingly or not at all. In one episode of *The OC*, for instance, the character Luke finds out that his father is gay. But the topic is not a regular feature of the show. Surprisingly perhaps, the gay theme appears most prominently in a drama aimed at pre-teens, *Degrassi*, which is produced in Canada and seen on Nickelodeon's sub-network The N. In the 2003 season one of the major characters, 10th grader Marco, came out of the closet and started dating Dylan, the older brother of his female friend Paige. The relationship became a major part of the series.

Indeed, television has changed a great deal since the 1950s days of *I Love Lucy*, when Ricky and Lucy Ricardo slept on separate beds divided by a nightstand even though they were married. Today, it is not unusual for television programs to show unmarried teenagers having sex. "Teenage Theresa tells a shocked Marissa that she is pregnant and can't afford to have a baby, and she doesn't have enough money for an abortion, but to Marissa the real tragedy is that Ryan might be the father," complains one PTC review that ranked a 2004 episode *The OC* as "Worst of the Week." It went on, "Underage drinking, teen sex and pregnancy, prostitution, strippers, and gambling are the laundry list of questionable themes that made up the plot on this teen-targeted show."

The PTC also found "profanities which are strong and frequent" on *One Tree Hill*. "Sex content is also what one might expect from this kind of 'modern' and 'hip' drama—discussions of 'porn names' in one episode, and an inappropriate scene in the premiere. Nathan, just stepping out of a shower in only in a pair of under-shorts, is followed by a girl wrapped only in a towel—who isn't even his girlfriend. His father sees them both and his reaction is one of surprise, yet, he takes no disciplinary action towards him."

Teen soap operas are not the only shows to push the limits. "Reality" shows like *The Surreal Life* or *The Bachelor* also attract a lot of teenage viewers—and also feature plenty of vulgar language and risqué scenes. A PTC study from 2004 found that over the 114.5 hours of "reality" television the group analyzed, there were

A publicity shot of the cast of *Dawson's Creek*, a popular drama on the WB network aimed at 13- to 18-year-olds. Organizations like the Parents Television Council (PTC) regularly panned the show because of its use of sexual situations and foul language.

1,135 instances of foul language and 492 "sexual situations or references." Among the objectionable scenes the PTC cited was a visit to a male strip club on *The Surreal Life* and another on *Survivor: Amazon* where women "take their bikini tops off and hold their hands over their bare breasts."

Violence, however, does not seem to be as much of a concern as sex on shows popular with teens. The PTC found 30 instances of violence on "reality" shows over the 114.5 hours it studied, far behind the sexual content. And in its reviews of teen dramas, the group says violence is for the most part relatively mild—little more than an occasional fistfight in shows like *One Tree Hill*.

Still, there is the increase in sexual language and in scenes involving teens and sex. What is the television industry's response? The Mediascope study said programming executives are split. Some believe young people should not be exposed to mature scenes, while others believe there is a need to "tell the whole story, to be honest and complete in reflecting social reality."

Whatever efforts Fox and WB make to attract teens—misguided or not—they face new competition from a fairly new kind of television media. A report in the Jack Myers newsletter that ranked Fox as the number one most frequently viewed network for teens also found that places two, three, and four (ahead of fifth-placed The WB) were all cable networks. So were 17 of the 21 top listings.

Cable's Fragmented Teens

Because there are so many channels, programmers on cable networks can do something their counterparts at over-the-air networks cannot—tailor their programming to narrow audiences. For sports fans, ESPN has at least four all-sports channels in English plus one in Spanish to compete with Fox Sports World, Fox Sports World en Español, and no less than 18 Fox mini-channels covering regional sports. News junkies have CNN, MSNBC, and Fox News. But that is just the start. Animal lovers? They have Animal Planet plus assorted wildlife documentaries on the Discovery Channel or the National Geographic Channel. Movies? One network runs only cowboy movies, another tear-jerking love stories, and yet another only science fiction films. History buffs have the History Channel and History International. There are networks dedicated to fitness buffs, golfers, outdoorsmen, home decorators, auto racing fans, and sophisticated lovers of fine food and wine.

And of course there are channels for teenagers. What is more, cable has become so specialized it has fragmented programming for young people according to age. There is the Disney Channel, with shows like *Lizzie McGuire* and *Kim Possible*, which are aimed at tweens and younger teenagers. Older teens watch MTV or its new competition, Fuse.

Those relatively small age gaps among teens do make for dissimilar viewing habits. A 2003 Gallup Youth Survey poll found that younger teens are likely to watch television more frequently than older teens. Among "light" viewers (those who said they watched TV one to five hours a week) 40 percent were in the 16–17 age range and 26 percent in the 13–15 range. Meanwhile among "heavy" viewers (those who said they watched 10 to 20 hours) younger kids outnumbered older ones 24 percent to 14 percent.

With those age differences in mind Viacom, the company that owns the CBS network as well as MTV, has created four distinct programming entities associated with the broader Nickelodeon brand. A pre-school child can start off watching *Oobi* on Noggin, graduate to *Blues Clues* on Nick Jr. around kindergarten, move on to the wisecracks of *Sponge Bob Square Pants* on Nickelodeon during grammar school, and grow up with *Degrassi* on The N as a tween in junior high. Then as teenagers they can get into *The Real World* or music videos on MTV, and eventually end up watching *CSI* on CBS as adults.

The strategy seems to be working, at least as far as attracting young people to cable. A Jack Myers study found in 2003 that only 52 percent of teens said they watched broadcast networks frequently, while 71 percent reported being frequent viewers of the cable networks.

The reason for the apparent preference, say cable executives, is clear. "Cable, with its ability to target, much more so than the broadcast approach, has developed a wantedness for teens and kids," Joe Ostrow of the Cabletelevision Advertising Bureau said. "The cable networks are brands that they identify with." That idea finds support in a Myers report that said 18 out of the 20 "most valued network brands" among teens were on cable, with only Fox and WB making the list, at next-to-last and last respectively. Whether on cable or broadcast, the largest media companies in the United States are paying attention to teens.

Chapter Three

Growing numbers of teenagers use the internet to find information, help with their homework, chat with friends via e-mail and instant messaging, and come into contact with a global online network of young people.

Teens and the Internet

When teens want to find out what time a movie is playing, they go to the Internet. When teens want to catch the latest sports scores, they go to the Internet. When teens want help with homework, they go to the Internet. They go to the Internet when they want to connect with friends, download music, shop for the latest fashions, read up on their favorite pop stars, or learn what languages are spoken in Senegal. Some teens even use the Internet to reveal their most personal secrets for the world to read.

"The Net is an AWESOME thing," said a 15-year-old boy quoted in *Teenage Life Online*, a study conducted by the Pew Internet and American Life Project. "Who would have thought that within the 20th century, a 'supertool' could be created, a tool that allows us to talk to people in other states without the long distance charges, a tool that allows us to purchase products without having to go to the store, a tool that gets information about almost any topic without having to go to the library. The Internet is an amazing invention, one that opens the door to mind-boggling possibilities. As a friend of mine would probably say, 'The Internet RULES!!!!!!!'"

The Internet has become such an important part of life for young people it is hard to believe that the World Wide Web, which along with e-mail ranks as the Internet's most popular feature, is barely a teenager too. What is now called the Internet was born in 1969 as a U.S. government-funded system called ARPANET, linking just four computers, at the University of California at Los Angeles (UCLA), the University of California at Santa Barbara, the University of Utah, and the Stanford Research Institute (SRI). The first Internet message, between UCLA and SRI, was also the first message that crashed.

For more than two decades after that only a handful of academics and computer experts ever went online. Logging on, sending e-mail, and digging out information required users to type in long strings of complicated commands. Then in 1991 a team at the European Particle Physics Laboratory (CERN) led by Tim Berners-Lee developed a system of connecting computers through *hyperlinks* they called the World Wide Web. Two years later Mosaic, the first *browser* with a *graphic interface*, made using the Web as easy as point-and-click. It was the start of a communications revolution. In Mosaic's first year Web traffic grew 341,634 percent, and in 1995 the Web bypassed "old Internet" services such as *FTP* and *Telnet*. Point-and-click e-mail programs became popular too, eliminating the need to learn yet another set of computer commands just to send a message to a friend.

It was around that time that young people started going online in large numbers. A 1995 Gallup survey found that 9 percent of teens said they had used the Internet the prior day, compared to 94

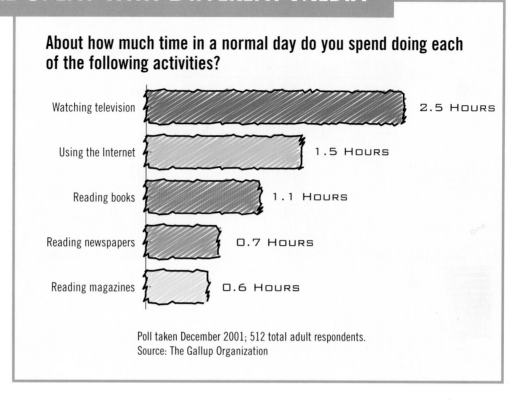

About how much time in a normal day do you spend doing each of the following activities?

Watching television	2.5 HOURS
Using the Internet	1.5 HOURS
Reading books	1.1 HOURS
Reading newspapers	0.7 HOURS
Reading magazines	0.6 HOURS

Poll taken December 2001; 512 total adult respondents.
Source: The Gallup Organization

percent who had listened to the radio and 93 percent that had watched television. By 1997 55 percent of teens said they had used the Internet at some point in their lives, even though only 29 percent had access to it at home.

Today the Internet is firmly set as a new form of mass media, joining television, radio, and print. In 2002 93 percent of teens told Gallup they used the Internet, and 86 percent said they had a computer at home. Gallup also found teens spend a substantial amount of time online. In a 2003 poll 38 percent of teens said they spent between one and five hours online each week, 16 percent said they spent five to ten hours online, and 7 percent reported spending more than ten hours. They all have at their fingertips a world of easily accessible information and ways to communicate. Ninety-six percent of teens in the latter survey said they use the

Teens and adults may have different views of the World Wide Web. The older generation may view the Internet as a tool, while young people see it as a source of entertainment.

Internet for e-mail or for finding information. Eighty-seven percent said they chat with friends with an instant messaging service. Seventy-three percent download music. Thirty-nine percent visit people they do not know in chat rooms, and thirty-one percent shop online.

Using the Internet has been a part of normal, everyday life as far back as most teenagers today can remember. If their grandparents were the first generation to grow up with radio, and their parents the first generation to grow up with television, teenagers of the millennium are the first Internet generation. One 2003 study conducted by Harris Interactive and Teenage Research Unlimited for Internet media company Yahoo found that young people aged

13 to 24 spend more time online each week than watching television, an average of 17 versus 14 hours, respectively. "Today's teens and young adults are not overwhelmed by the abundance of media choices . . . but rather feel empowered by it and are able to multi-task," says the report. Wenda Harris Millard, an executive at Yahoo!, added that the Internet has become the center of teens' media activity. "[The Internet] is a primary medium for information, product information, pricing information, school needs. . . . It would never occur to them to go to a newspaper to look up a movie time."

Internet use among the young is likely to keep growing. Jupiter Research predicts there will be 22 million American teens online by 2008, up from 18 million in 2003. Even the very young are going online: fully 35 percent of kids 2 to 5 years of age in the U.S. use the Internet, says a 2003 report by the Corporation for Public Broadcasting. With its tremendous popularity, teens' Internet use raises several questions. Where do young people go on the Web? How do they use e-mail, instant messaging, and chat rooms to connect with friends or even strangers? Why do so many create their own *blogs* and write about issues ranging from politics to their personal lives? And how wide is the divide between the digital "haves" and "have nots"?

Surfing the Web, Teen Style

When that 96 percent of teens told Gallup they use the Internet for "finding information," it is a sure bet that the vast majority looked for that information by surfing on the World Wide Web. Several studies have found that teens use the Internet to find help with their homework more often than they do to find out about music, sports, or fashion. In a 2003 report by the Kaiser Family

Foundation, 94 percent of teens said they have used the Internet to research schoolwork, compared to the 85 percent who used it to get "information on movies, music or TV." Eighty-one percent said they went online to play games, 78 percent to get news, 50 percent for sports scores, and 36 percent to buy something. Another study, by the Pew Foundation, found an even larger gap (although the question was worded differently): once again, 94 percent of teens said they used the Web for schoolwork, while 54 percent said they surfed "to keep up with trends in fashion and music."

But maybe it is not so surprising, given that 99 percent of American schools are wired to the Internet. Gallup found that there are 3.8 school computers per student in the U.S., compared to 125 computers per student twenty years ago. The 2003 Gallup survey also showed 28 percent of teens graded the technology available at their schools as an A, 33 percent gave it a B, and 25 percent gave it a C. Eight percent gave their schools' technology a D, and 5 percent gave it a failing grade.

Budget shortages that prevent schools from getting the very latest technology, combined with teens' savvy understanding of the very same advances, may account for the relative dissatisfaction, Gallup says. Yet even with older technology Internet access at schools is so widespread that the Web is beginning to replace the old-fashioned library as a research tool. Seventy-one percent of teens in the Pew study said they rely mostly on the Web to do research for school, compared with 24 percent that reported using mostly the library and 4 percent that used both equally. "I find the Internet most useful when I need help for school," maintained a 15-year-old boy. "Without the Internet you need to go to the library and walk around looking for books. In today's world you can just go home and get into the Internet and type in your search

Overall, how many hours per week do you spend on the Internet?

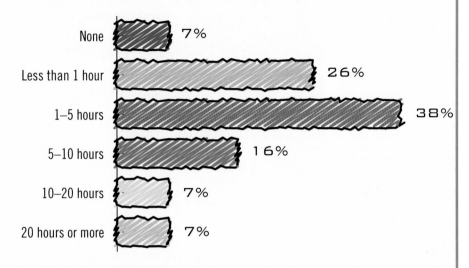

None	7%
Less than 1 hour	26%
1–5 hours	38%
5–10 hours	16%
10–20 hours	7%
20 hours or more	7%

What do teens who are on the Internet more than five hours a week do when they are online?

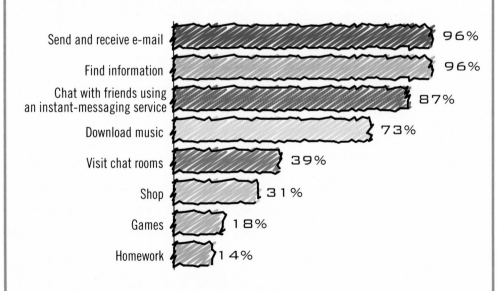

Send and receive e-mail	96%
Find information	96%
Chat with friends using an instant-messaging service	87%
Download music	73%
Visit chat rooms	39%
Shop	31%
Games	18%
Homework	14%

Poll taken January–February 2003; 1,200 total respondents age 13–17.
Source: Gallup Youth Survey/The Gallup Organization

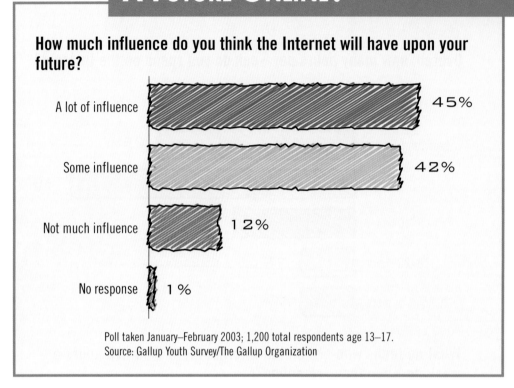

How much influence do you think the Internet will have upon your future?

A lot of influence	45%
Some influence	42%
Not much influence	12%
No response	1%

Poll taken January–February 2003; 1,200 total respondents age 13–17.
Source: Gallup Youth Survey/The Gallup Organization

term. The results are endless. There is so much information that you have to ignore a lot of it."

There is plenty of reference material online that can make some trips to the library unnecessary. Users need to be make sure, however, that the information they find comes from a reliable, credible website, because just about anybody can say just about anything online. Another limitation of the Internet is that most books—fiction as well as nonfiction, the classics as well as newer works—are not available online, at least not as part of the free-of-charge Internet. So the library with its "old fashioned" books, are still necessary resources for any educated person.

Still, it seems that fast Internet connections make for better students. The CPB study found that among teens whose families switched from a *dial-up* connection to *broadband,* 23 percent reported getting better grades — even though just 13 percent of parents expected that broadband would result in better grades. "More time online (which broadband seems to enable) does not inevitably lead to children abandoning their schoolwork," the report added. "Not only do parents greatly value the educational benefits of the Internet, but their children take advantage of them."

How Teens Use the Internet

Of course, those sites that help with research for school are not necessarily the best liked destinations. The most popular are websites designed for teens' non-academic interests. According to "Teensites.com," a study by the Center for Media Education, music sites were the most popular. Sixty-eight percent of teens mentioned them, followed by sites about movies (54 percent), relationships (52 percent), advice (49 percent), and fashion (43 percent). At the low end of the popularity scale were sites focusing on religion (16 percent), travel (11.1 percent), food (11.1 percent), volunteerism (11.1 percent), the environment (6.2 percent), and nature (2.5 percent). Said the report, "The online teen culture foregrounds entertainment over information. The lion's share of teen Web site content revolves around the popular culture that young people so avidly consume as well as the personal issues that tend to be foremost in their minds."

What does it all add up to? One 17-year old quoted by Pew researchers reported surfing the Web "just looking for stuff that interests me at new sites." In other words, to have fun. The study found that 84 percent of teens go online for that purpose, compared to 63 percent of adults. On the Web, teens are also more likely than adults to look for information about movies or other leisure activities (83 percent to 65 percent), play or download games (66 percent to 34 percent), and check sports scores (47 percent to 38 percent). In contrast, teenagers are less likely than adults to research a new product (66 percent to 77 percent) or actually buy something online (31 percent to 53 percent).

"Teens and adults (particularly parents) use the Internet for different reasons," the study concluded. "Both groups appreciate the communication tools of the Internet. Youth are more interested in entertainment activities or information and parents lean more toward online tasks like transactions and information searches that will help their families like seeking health and medical material." Only 26 percent of teens researched health issues online, compared to 57 percent of adults.

There are also some differences between the way teenage boys and teenage girls use the Web, Pew found. Girls are more likely than boys to look for dieting, health, or fitness information (30 percent to 22 percent). Boys are more likely to research items to buy (77 percent to 55 percent) and sports scores. Still, when looking at the overall most popular reasons to surf the Web—such as doing it for fun or to visit websites about movies, TV shows, music groups, or pop stars—the study did not find much difference between the habits of males and females.

Sexual Issues

Another activity in which Web-surfing boys and girls participate pretty much equally is to "go online to find information that is hard to talk about with other people." Although only 18 percent of all teens told Pew they did that, teens will have no trouble finding sites that offer frank talk about teenage relationships and sexual issues. "You may have noticed that I often note the website virtualkid.com," said a 16-year-old boy in the Pew study. "It was a website for teens complete with forums and information and just help in general for teenagers. . . . Besides dating, the site had information on puberty and all the awkward teenage moments. It was a really nice, helpful site." A 17-year old added, "If I did need to find such information at a point in my life my first step would be looking online. It's easier, more private, and faster. Then if I could not find what I was looking for, I'd head to a library or see a professional. I figure that if you can solve a personal problem yourself, more power to you."

Libraries, schools, and other organizations providing web content to young people often use filters to prevent them from finding explicitly sexual or violent content online. However, groups like the American Civil Liberties Union (ACLU) argue that such filters also block legitimate and valuable sites and violate the Constitution's First Amendment right to free speech.

Of course, not every website that covers teens and sex is equally valid. It is not difficult for a young person searching for the answer to a sincere question about a sexual issue to end up, even accidentally, on one of the many pornographic websites all over the Internet. The Kaiser Family Foundation reports that 70 percent of teens ages 15 to 17 say they have accidentally come across pornography online. Nearly a quarter (23 percent) say this happens "very" or "somewhat" often.

The use of filters provides one way to stay out of inappropriate websites. Seventy-six percent of 15- to 17-year-olds who have Internet access at school say computers there have filters that block access to adult content, according to Kaiser, and approximately one-third say they have a filter on home computers. Sometimes filters go overboard: 46 percent say they have been blocked from a non-pornographic site.

For some parents, however, Internet filters alone are not enough. "Yes, I do have two teenagers (a boy and girl). I have had to deal with all the issues related to the 'stuff' on the Net," a father from Georgia wrote on www.netfamilynews.org. "I have always taken the approach of open conversation with my kids. It's important to note that, in addition to Web content, our kids are exposed to a tremendous amount of things that challenge us. Just flipping the channels on TV can take you to explicit material on HBO, MTV, Howard Stern, and much more. . . . We have never used filters in our home. I prefer to have open conversations and dialogue."

How many parents monitor their kids' online activities? The trend seems to be that mom and dad are more likely to check on younger kids than teenagers. According to the Kaiser report 76 percent of children ages 6 to 12 say an adult is "usually in the same room or nearby when they go online at home," compared to just

35 percent of teens who say the same thing. There is also disagreement about how much parental involvement there really is. "A majority of parents say they enforce time limits on Internet use, surf together, and check up on sites their children have visited," says the Kaiser study, "but most teens say they do not have time limits or go online with their parents, and less than one-third believe that their parents have ever checked."

Online Diaries and Blogs

One mother from Washington, D.C., who posted a question on www.netfamilynews.org did check, and did not like what she found. "I am trying to find information about OpenDiary.com," she wrote. "My daughter has used the site to post diary entries, and I am uncomfortable with that because I discovered that anyone can get to her entries and post reactions."

That mom was concerned about a fairly new Internet phenomenon: The online diary or "blog," (short for Web log). Generations of teenagers have written their innermost thoughts on the pages of diaries, then locked them away from the eyes of parents and even their best friends. Diaries were not meant for anyone other than the writer to read. But their modern-day digital counterparts can be just as personal—with the difference that they can be read by just about anyone across the globe with a computer and Internet access.

To be sure, some blogs focus on social or political issues. Like a newspaper columnist, teens that write such blogs can express their opinions to the entire world. Others teens write about their favorite musician or pop star, whether on a "regular" website or a blog in which new entries are posted most days. Still other blogs cover mundane details of everyday life. "Work is still stupid busy," reads the May 26, 2004, entry of one blogger. "I complain about work a lot but other than my family and soccer, work is next in line! yea, i know, not even friends. It's pretty bad!"

Then there are the ones that reveal deeply personal struggles. "I feel so freakin' depressed today and I have no reason to," reads the online diary of a California teen. "I think it might be because I haven't had my Trazodone in the last two nights so I am moderately sleep deprived. I seriously can't wait till summer when I won't have to be around [his hometown] anymore. Being there reminds me of the bad things that have happened recently. I hope that I have a better year when I go to [college] in the fall. I am so tired of being depressed."

No one really knows how many blogs there are. The Pew study said that among teen Internet users 19 percent of girls and 29 percent of boys have created their own website, and Jupiter Research estimates that 30 percent of teenagers use "personal pages and weblogs," without distinguishing between the two. But there is a difference between a full-fledged personal Web page and a blog. Making a website requires some knowledge of technology to design it and upload it—aside from text, websites can have content such as graphics and video clips. But a blog does not have to require anything more than typing words, because sites such as www.teenopendiary.com or www.diaryland.com offer ready-made space to teens without a lot of technological skills. They only need to write their thoughts and send them in as easily as sending a friend an e-mail.

Except that it will not be just one recipient who can read it. "Online diaries are rapidly becoming another way that teenagers talk among themselves about themselves," said a story in the *Washington Post.* "More permanent than instant messages and more accessible than chat rooms, these diaries give them a forum for expression that is anonymous in origin (screen names only) and international in audience."

The increasing interest of blogs and online dairies raises concerns about privacy and even safety. Family internet experts at www.netfamilynews.org advised the worried mother from Washington, "What's extremely important for your daughter to be

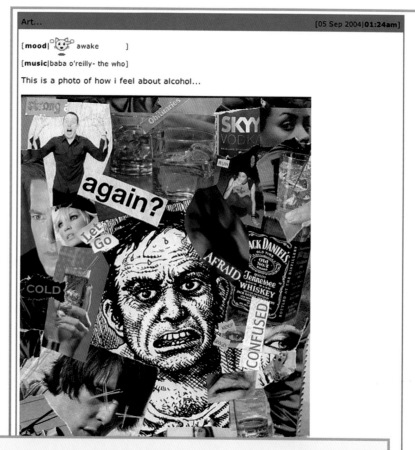

This collage is an example of an online journal entry. Writers can post text, photos, or artwork, and others can comment on their posting. Some people believe these journals serve as a healthy outlet for teen emotions, yet parents often worry that their children may be allowing strangers to see too much of their personal lives.

aware of for her own protection in any community site is that . . . she must never post any personally identifiable information—last name, phone number, school name, address, or even town. By "posting" we mean within diary entries and in user profiles (it's best to leave profiles blank). Ideally, screen names don't even give away a user's gender."

The mom responded, "I gather that part of the thrill of this type of site is hearing from lots of other people, [but] it really is not safe for teens to talk to people they don't know. However, teens generally don't seem to see it that way and think that they will never get into trouble—just like they think they will never get into a car accident if they drive just a bit too fast or recklessly."

Keeping in touch

Relatively few online teens have blogs. Nearly all of them, however, use e-mail or instant messaging to stay in touch with friends. According to a Gallup Youth Survey poll conducted in 2003, 86 percent of teens said they used e-mail and 65 percent said they used an instant messaging service. Among teens who spend five or more hours a week online, the use of those two services rises even higher: 96 percent said they used e-mail and 87 percent said they used instant messaging. Another Gallup poll, taken the year before, found girls were more likely than boys to use e-mail. Seventy-six percent of girls said they e-mailed friends the past week, compared to 65 percent of boys.

Although there may be a difference between teen boys and teen girls in how often they use e-mail, there is not much difference between the e-mail use of teens overall and their parents. After all, many adults use e-mail every day in their jobs. But when it comes to instant messaging, it is a teenage world. The Pew study found a gap of 30 percentage points in the number of teens who use instant messaging compared to adults.

"Many American youth say that Internet communication, especially instant messaging, has become an essential feature of their social lives," says the Pew report. "For them, face-to-face interaction and some telephone conversations have been partially replaced with email and instant message communication. Relationships that once might have withered are now nourished by the ease and speed of instant message exchanges and email messages." The report continues, "Instant messaging has permeated teen culture to such an extent that for some 'message me later' has replaced 'call me.'"

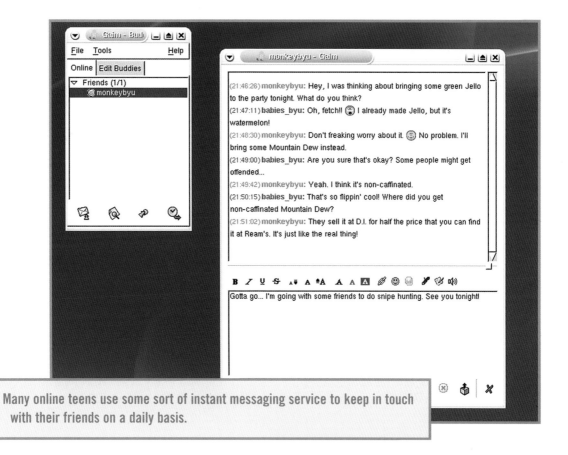

Many online teens use some sort of instant messaging service to keep in touch with their friends on a daily basis.

Many teens—90 percent, according to Pew—use instant messaging to stay in touch with friends who live far away. "My buddy list includes friends from school, past teachers, family members or family friends, and friends that I have met that don't go to my school but [who] I like to keep in touch with, especially friends from camp [from] the previous summers," said a 16-year-old girl in an e-mail message to the Pew Internet Project.

Those buddy lists also includes friends who live nearby, with whom teens share the latest school gossip. Forty-eight percent of them told the Pew survey that their relationships have improved

A DIGITAL DIVIDE?

Social scientists have said there is in the United States what they call a "digital divide" between those who use the Internet and those who do not, based to some extent on race and to some extent on family income.

A report by the Corporation for Public Broadcasting (CPB) found that in 2002 87 percent of white non-Hispanic families (regardless of income) had a computer at home compared to 71 percent of black families and 69 percent of Hispanic families. In addition, 98 percent of high-income families (regardless of ethnicity) had a home computer compared to 65 percent of low-income families. As the numbers show, the gap is wider when taking income into account than it is when considering ethnicity.

Other studies show that differences in the *way* that some ethnic groups use the Internet are perhaps related to income differences between those ethnic groups. A 2003 Gallup survey showed black teens and Hispanic teens were slightly less likely than non-Hispanic white teens to say that they use the Internet for e-mail (89 percent to as a result, with more than six in ten of the heavy users saying that the Internet has helped them to enhance old friendships. Also, dating couples have started and stopped their relationship through instant messaging. Seventeen percent of teens surveyed by Pew have used an instant message to ask someone out on a date, and 13 percent have broken up by this mode of communication. The report tells of a 16–year-old boy who said of his new girlfriend, "She and I started to talk online and played a game where we could ask each other anything. I eventually asked her out . . . online, of course. It's not the most romantic thing to do, but I was very nervous and it helped to make it a little bit easier."

Even kids with few friends use instant messaging to make up for

78 percent) or instant messaging (70 percent to 56 percent). Yet the gap almost disappeared when teens were asked about using the Internet for things that do not involve an immediate social network, such as finding information (93 percent non-Hispanic white to 92 percent black and Hispanic).

"The implication is that minority teens who do have Internet access are no less likely to use it per se—that is, they have no less inherent interest in the Web," Gallup concluded. "But, given that they remain more likely to fall into lower socioeconomic levels, they may have smaller networks of close friends and family capable of receiving e-mail or instant messages."

Yet there is good news. Between 2000 and 2002, says the CPB report, African-American kids increased their Internet access by 205 percent and access for low-income children grew by 96 percent, a much faster pace than for whites or high-income teens (the study did not measure the growth rate for Hispanics). So the trend seems to be toward narrowing the Digital Divide.

the social life they may not have offline, says UCLA social scientist Elisheva Gross. "I've always been very shy in real life," noted one 16-year-old boy who was quoted by Pew. "I'm home-schooled, and have avoided most contact with children my own age. The Internet has, in many ways, replaced real-life socialization for me. This is abnormal, but I don't think its 'bad' by any means. I've become comfortable with socializing both on-line and off and I've made a large number of friends by participating in small on-line communities."

For shy teens, it may be easier to chat on instant messaging than speak face-to-face. "Online teens appreciate instant messaging because they say it gives them a greater freedom to craft arguments carefully or to word an unpleasant message delicately," noted the Pew study. As one 17-year-old girl put it, "It is easier to talk to someone about certain topics online, than to talk about them face-to-face. Online you can think things over, and erase them before you look stupid, rather than to their face, where you can't always take things back."

Still, 67 percent of teens said instant messaging does not help when trying to make new friends. "One person I met [online] was about to move to our town, so he IM-ed me [sent an instant message]," said one 16-year-old boy quoted in the Pew study. "When he moved here I kinda showed him around. It was ok, but I really did not like him. He was a little too shy, a year younger than I and incessantly irritating. I would prefer not to have a repeat." The experience was unpleasant for all concerned. But sometimes meeting someone new online can have more serious consequences.

Chatting With Dangerous Strangers

In March 2003, 14-year-old Jeanne Rohrig and 15-year-old Whitney Irvin were reported missing from their homes in

Kentucky. A week later they were found in California, lured there by a man they had met in an Internet chat room who sent them bus tickets, false identification, and money. Police say the man, Kevin Gibbs of Fresno, intended to use the girls as prostitutes. The two Kentucky teens were fortunate that they used Gibbs' cell phone to call their hometown. Authorities traced the phone call and located the girls, and police arrested the man who had endangered their lives. Other teens have not been so fortunate.

```
103 [2:00 PM]:        HI
 [2:00 PM]:      HI Craig, what's up?
103 [2:00 PM]:        NOTHING MUCH ASL
103 [2:00 PM]:        ASL PLSE
 [2:01 PM]:      15 female fort lauderdale
103 [2:01 PM]:        COOL
 [2:01 PM]:      how bout u asl?
103 [2:01 PM]:        SAME BUT MALE AND UK
 [2:01 PM]:      really 15?
103 [2:02 PM]:        YEAH
 [2:02 PM]:      sorry, lookin for someone older
103 [2:02 PM]:        OH
```

Chatting with strangers on the internet can be dangerous, as sometime adults pretend to be teenagers in order to lure unsuspecting young people into meeting them. This is a screen shot of a conversation in which a law-enforcement officer trolling the web for internet predators is contacted (the unknown messenger's comments are in blue highlighted type).

A 2003 Gallup poll found that 26 percent of all teenagers surveyed, and 39 percent of those who are online at least five hours a week, admitted to contacting strangers in chat rooms. What is more, Gallup also found that teens who chat with strangers were more likely than those who do not to engage in other risky behavior. Thirty-five percent of teens who chatted with people they did not know used alcohol, compared to 28 percent of teens who did not talk to online strangers. Similarly, they were more likely to have tried marijuana (29 percent to 17 percent) and smoked cigarettes (11 percent to 7 percent).

Is this a mere coincidence? "One of the eternal maxims of survey research is that 'correlation does not prove causality,'" says a Gallup analysis of the survey. "Are visits to chat rooms causing teens to experiment with drugs, or might there be something else at work that causes teens both to visit strangers in chat rooms and experiment with drugs? We can't answer this question, but Gallup's data do suggest that chatting with strangers on the Internet may be part of a larger group of unhealthy and possibly reckless behaviors for some teens. Parents would be well advised to monitor their kids' online activities."

Parents are indeed concerned. According to a Pew study, 57 percent of parents worry "some" or "a lot" that their children will be contacted by strangers online. Yet 28 percent of teens said they do not worry about it at all, while an additional 37 percent of teens worry about it only "a little."

Still, that does not necessarily mean that teenagers are reckless about meeting in person people that they have first chatted with online. Betsy Van Dorn, in an article titled "Protecting Teens in Online Chat Rooms" at www.familyeducation.com, urges parents to monitor their teens' online travels but adds, "Here are some responses that lead me to believe teenagers have more common sense than they're given credit for:

"Beware of weirdos! Talk to him on the telephone!"

"Bring along a friend or two."

"Get permission from your parents."

"Meet in a crowded place. Don't go alone."

"Go ahead, but go with your parents."

Of course, it is hard to envision a teenager asking mom or dad to come along to meet an Internet stranger. Yet at the same time, most teenagers do not run out to meet every stranger they meet in chat rooms. Most remain exactly that—strangers in chat rooms, locked away in the digital safety of the computer teens so love to use.

Chapter Four

The Beatles prepare to perform on the *Ed Sullivan Show*, February 1964. Popular music has been an important element of the youth culture in the United States since the 1950s.

Teens' Musical Culture

"The United States is now in the midst of one of those remarkable phenomena of mass hysteria which occur from time to time on this side of the Atlantic," a British newspaper reported in 1945. "Mr. Frank Sinatra, an amiable young singer of popular songs, is inspiring extraordinary personal devotion on the part of many thousands of young people, and particularly young girls between the ages of, say, twelve and eighteen."

It was the age of the "bobby-soxers," girls who wore saddle shoes with short white stockings and swooned over crooners like Frank Sinatra. This "mass hysteria" was only possible because of the mass media—such outlets as the radio stations that played Sinatra's music and the gossip magazines that breathlessly chronicled every aspect of the star's life. But there was a difference between the bobby-soxers of the 1940s and teens today. Although Sinatra was popular among young people, he was also popular with their parents. Back then, there was no divide between music for adults and music for teens. They liked many of the same tunes. In fact, what is now known as youth culture did not exist then. The very word "teenager" only began to be used that same decade.

"Before World War II, Americans went from childhood to adulthood in short order—children were considered fit for work and marriage once puberty was complete," explains George H. Gallup. "But with the great surge of prosperity after the war, most middle-class teens did not need to work. They had more leisure time and more money to spend." Television and, even more so, radio took notice. Gallup continued, "Advertisers coveted them; rock and roll defined them, and sociologists began to study them. A distinct youth culture was born, and the American teenager was here to stay."

What is that distinct youth culture? It has to do with an attitude of rebelliousness, of challenging the established order of the adult world. And it revolves around music, which as Gallup noted even today still defines youth culture.

The first star of the teen era was Elvis Presley. Parents never viewed Sinatra, the teen idol that preceded Presley, with much alarm. After all, adults liked him too. But Presley's sneering smile and gyrating hips scandalized the older generation. In one early appearance on Ed Sullivan's television show, the camera dared show him only from the waist up. It was too much for older people, but teenagers loved it. They embraced rock 'n' roll and they did so as part of their own identity, separate from that of adults. Society in general also began to view teens as a group apart, with its own view of the world.

Music for young people became even more entrenched in the decades that followed as rockers led the way in setting what was "cool"—not only in music but in clothing, hairstyle, and even politics. Screaming girls welcomed the Beatles to the United States in 1964, while boys copied their mop-topped hairdos. They were forerunners of the "British Invasion," and soon the popularity of other British rock groups like the Rolling Stones and the Who exploded among American teens.

By the late 1960s, young people began to take themselves more seriously, challenging long-established moral and political values of society. Many young people, inspired by the music of the period, protested against the Vietnam War, tried drugs, and launched the sexual revolution. They saw their efforts as liberating, while adults saw it as a dangerous rejection of traditional values.

The importance of music to the youth culture of the United States continued with the 1970s heyday of heavy metal groups such as Led Zeppelin and the birth of "punk" groups like the Ramones and the Sex Pistols. In the 1980s Bruce Springsteen's songs about blue-collar alienation gave youth culture a distinctive working-class political edge, and in that same decade MTV was born.

The birth of MTV marked the media's acceptance that youth music and youth culture had, in a way, matured. No longer was it relegated to specialized radio stations and the occasional guest appearance of a rock group on television variety shows. Now, young people had a television network they could call their own. The music videos MTV constantly played helped make youth culture even more widespread. Soon bands did not just make records, they were also expected to make videos. Their music—whether it was rock, rap, grunge, pop, or some other form—along with the fashions and rebellious attitudes each genre inspired, were now on television every hour of every day for the world to see.

Today, many popular bands have an strong influence on teens. The group Green Day, for example, encouraged young people to vote in the 2004 presidential election, and a record number of 18- to 20-year-old voters turned out.

Today, the music of popular musicians is fresh and different from that of the youth idols that preceded them—yet in a way it is the same, because like Presley, the Beatles, or Nirvana, new stars continue to inspire youth and worry adults. Still, the gyrating hips that shocked parents in the 1950s seem mild compared to the antics of modern music videos. Artists today regularly write lyrics that include explicit sexual content and the rawest of vulgarities. Each generation, it seems, needs to go further than the previous one in order for its signature songs to scandalize adults.

For the most part, however, listeners can only hear the explicit language on the CD recordings they play themselves at home or in cars. Facing the threat of fines of up to $3 million from the Federal Communications Commission (FCC) for airing indecent lyrics, nearly all media censor the most objectionable lyrics, from MTV to local radio stations. Besides, not all teenagers are happy with the proliferation of "dirty words." According to a 2002 Gallup Poll, almost one-fifth of teens between the ages of 13 and 17 said they never using profane language, and 80 percent said their parents should not curse around their families. The survey also detected differences according to social class. "Twenty-four percent of blue-collar teens say they always avoid foul language," Gallup found. "The offspring of white-collar workers are less likely to resist the temptation—only 14 percent say they never swear"

Ironically the youth culture that produced such lyrics would not have even existed without a mass media to publicize it. Radio, teen magazines, and television shows have helped promote the fashions, attitudes, music, and celebrities that teens call their own—whether it was Presley and slicked-back hair in the 1950s, the Beatles and bell-bottoms in the 1960s, or MTV and hip-hop today. But at the start of it all, there was radio.

Radio, Always Radio

When an unknown television network called MTV made its debut on August 1, 1981, on a little used medium called cable television, the first music video it played was for a song called "Video Killed the Radio Star." No doubt, executives at the fledgling channel knew they were onto a revolutionary concept for teen viewers. The network's very name, spelled out, said it all: "Music TV" combined two things that teens were crazy about—music, and television. There was speculation at the time that songs with video were going to doom radio.

Nothing of the sort happened. More than two decades later 89 percent of teens said in a Gallup survey they had listened to music on the radio the previous day. Broken down by gender, that figure includes 83 percent of boys surveyed and 96 percent of girls. What is more, only 59 percent said they had watched music videos on television, with girls once again outscoring boys, 67 percent to 51 percent.

The reason video did not replace radio may be that the audio-only nature of radio lets busy teens do other things when listening—something that is more difficult when they are watching television. Even in today's sound- and image-saturated world teens often attend to other media with the radio on. A 2003 study by Arbitron, a radio marketing firm, found that 64 percent of kids surveyed age 13 to 17 said they listened to radio while chatting with instant messages, 74 percent said they did it while reading, and 79 percent while working on their computers or surfing the Web. Thirty-four percent said they watch TV and listen to radio at the same time.

Teen Radio Today

Teens can find the most youth-oriented music stations on the FM band. Young people ages 15 to 17 listen to the radio an average of one hour and 45 minutes each day, according to Arbitron. They are most likely to listen in the early morning before leaving for school and again around 3 P.M. after they get home. During summer vacation, peak hours are in the mid-afternoon.

What they listen to has changed since the days when AM stations played top 40 hits and FM stations played rock. Now, music radio programmers tailor their play lists to particular audiences, similar to the way cable networks try to attract specific demographics. To figure out who is listening to what, radio executives

Radio has remained an important part of many teens' lives. One reason it is popular is that teens can do other things while listening to music or programs.

The types of radio shows teenagers listen to have changed over the years. While some teens prefer stations that play their favorite genres of music, others tune in to controversial talk-radio hosts like Howard Stern.

use a calculation they call "Persons Using Radio," or PUR. It measures the percentage of people listening to some form of radio at one particular time.

Using PUR and focusing on young people in metropolitan Philadelphia (a location that makes the measurement indicative of listenership in large cities and their suburbs, but not of rural areas) Arbitron found that the least popular music format for teens among the four formats in the study was the mellow "Adult Contemporary," where play lists includes ballads by artists ranging from Gloria Estefan to Shania Twain. Just 0.7 percent of kids 12 to 14 in the Philadelphia region were listening to stations that played such music when the survey was conducted in late 2003. The format did almost as poorly with older teens, as just one percent of youths age 15 to 17 tuned in on average.

Also not popular with either age group were AOR or "Album Oriented Rock" stations, which play the kind of music teens' Boomer parents might have listened to in the 1970s. Just 1.2 percent of Philadelphia tweens were listening on average, and 1.9 percent of the older teens.

Both age groups were equally likely to listen to stations that play "Contemporary Hit Radio," or CHR, a diverse format that can range from the rock-pop of Avril Lavigne to the soul-pop of Alicia Keys. Two percent of Philadelphia's 12- to 17-year-olds teens were tuned in to that kind of music during the average 15 minutes that week. In contrast the "Urban" format, heavy on rap and hip-hop, had the largest discrepancy between the two age groups. Only 1.2 percent of 'tweens were listening compared to 2.3 of older teens, for whom it was the most popular format.

Whatever the mix, teens continue to listen to the radio. Seventy-seven percent of them do it every day, a 2004 Gallup poll found. Radio will likely continue to fill a central role in shaping teens' musical tastes—at the same time that teens' musical tastes will continue to shape the radio industry.

Music Downloads

Once upon a time teens who liked a song they heard on the radio went to stores and bought the artist's albums. A few years later, they bought cassette tapes; later, they purchased CDs. These days, however, many teens prefer to download their music online—sometimes paying for it, sometimes not.

The height of the music download craze was in the late 1990s, when the popular program Napster allowed home computers to connect to one another directly through the Internet and exchange music files. A person in California could digitally swap favorite tunes with someone in New

York—or with a person in Mexico or Germany, for that matter. Literally an entire world of free music was available.

The trouble was that the artists who wrote and played the songs were not getting paid, and neither were record companies. After decades of steady growth, shipments of CDs to music stores dropped from 942.5 million in 2000 to 735.9 million in 2003. This caused the Recording Industry Association of America (RIAA), a trade group that represents U.S. record companies, to take legal action to shut down Napster and sue users who download music without paying for it.

Yet teens did not stop—47 percent of kids aged 13 to 17 told Gallup pollsters in 2003 that they use the Internet for downloading songs. As a result, record companies, giant technology firms such as Apple, and even some smaller Websites began to offer music downloads for a fee—as little as 99 cents for a song as opposed to the $15 or $16 that a CD costs in a store.

Teens, record companies, and artists all seem to agree that the Internet has irreversibly changed the way people acquire music. Yet there is disagreement about how much songs should cost, if anything. For instance, a 2003 Gallup survey found that 83 percent of teens said they believed it is morally acceptable to download "music from the Internet for free." An earlier poll found that as many teens admitted to downloading music without paying as admitted to having cheated on a test, yet only 18 percent said the latter was morally acceptable.

"I think downloading music from the Internet is morally acceptable because it's the same thing as taping a song from the radio—no one is getting hurt. But cheating on a test is getting help from an outside source without studying and learning the material," explained Elizabeth, a 17-year-old high school junior. "So

Do you use the Internet for downloading music?

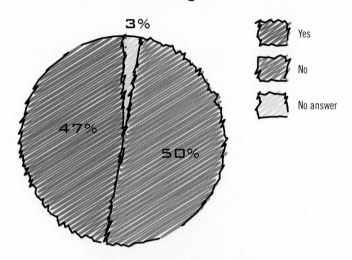

Percentage of downloaders; classified by gender and race.

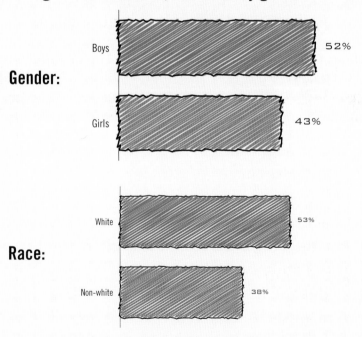

Poll taken January–February 2003; 1,200 total respondents age 13–17.
Source: Gallup Youth Survey/The Gallup Organization

Lars Ulrich of Metallica exchanges angry words with Hank Barry (right), CEO of Napster, at a July 2000 hearing before the Senate Judiciary Committee on musical copyright and the internet. The battle over online music-sharing programs and downloads of MP3-encoded songs remains very sensitive. Musicians argue that free downloads hurt sales of their CDs, while others believe that it helps promote the artists.

you're not only harming yourself, but possibly your classmates, as well, by creating a false curve."

Another teenager insisted to Gallup that "downloading music is theft and theft is morally wrong. Just because you're not walking into a store and grabbing a CD from the shelf, it's still wrong. It's hurting the record industry and the artists who make the music." Yet he added, "But will it stop me from downloading? No way."

Why do so many teens think it is fine to get music they do not pay for, and for which musicians will not get paid? "I suspect the largest moral issue is simply the old beach-combing, law-of-the-sea, finders-keepers mentality," Rushworth Kidder, president of the Institute for Global Ethics in Camden, Maine, told the Gallup Organization. "[Teens think,] 'If something falls overboard into the great sea of the Internet and washes up on my computer—hey, it's there, isn't it?"

What is more, a majority of Americans does not believe free music downloads hurt record sales. "Seventy-nine percent say the fact that music can be shared and copied over the Internet has no effect on their likelihood to purchase CDs, and another 8 percent say they are actually *more* likely to buy CDs because of file-sharing," Gallup reported in 2002. Teens surveyed the year before had a different view, however. Fifty-five percent said people would be "less likely" to purchase music, and 44 percent said "more likely."

Gallup also found that boys appear to be more likely to use the Internet for downloading music (52 percent) than girls (43 percent), and that regardless of gender, non-Hispanic, white teens are more likely music downloaders than Hispanic and black teens (53 percent to 38 percent respectively).

Chapter Five

A young man reads a newspaper on his way to school. The number of teen newspaper readers has fallen in recent years. This has inspired some papers to make a greater effort to reach out to young readers.

Teens and Newspapers

Sixteen-year-old Matthew Moran reads a newspaper almost every day. But like many teenagers, Matthew does not usually go beyond a quick scan of the headlines. "Most of the stories aren't really appealing," he said. "I'll read it if a teacher gives an assignment." Yet Matthew says he does keep up with what is going on in the United States and the world. He discusses current events with his father, he watches television newscasts, and he follows the news online.

Studies show Matthew's newsgathering habits are typical of American teenagers. Although many teens read newspapers, growing numbers are getting their news about the world from other sources, such as the magazines, radio, and the Internet. News industry experts say that the number of teen newspaper readers is declining. This downward trend poses a challenge to editors: how can they convince more teens to read newspapers?

"The younger generation is crucially important to newspapers in part because it is so large," *Washington Post* managing editor Steve Coll told Harvard University's Nieman Foundation for Journalism. There are more than 28 million teens in the United States, says the 2000 U.S. Census. And getting more teen readers now will be important to the survival of newspapers in the long term, because readership habits are formed at an early age. Editors hope that young people who become regular readers today will stick with the newspaper as they get older, becoming the adult readers of tomorrow. They worry that a decline in readership among today's teens might eventually threaten the very existence of newspapers.

But attracting teen readers is no easy task. Editors of mainstream dailies do not want to turn their publications into teen publications with such a strong focus on youth that older readers are turned off. Yet at the same time many editors acknowledge that to appeal to young people, something has to change.

Some newspapers have begun to be more conscious of finding stories not merely about teens but also for teens. There is also a move toward the kind of edgy, shorter stories teens say they like—sometimes in stories that appear in the main sections of a paper, but also increasingly in special sections aimed at a younger readership.

Stories For Teens

Teens have long complained newspapers are "uncool." In 1990 media expert Cathy J. Cobb-Walgren studied why teenagers believed newspapers were old fashioned. She learned that teenagers thought newspapers did not have enough stories about their interests and hobbies. Teens say editors do not even consider what kinds of stories young people like to read.

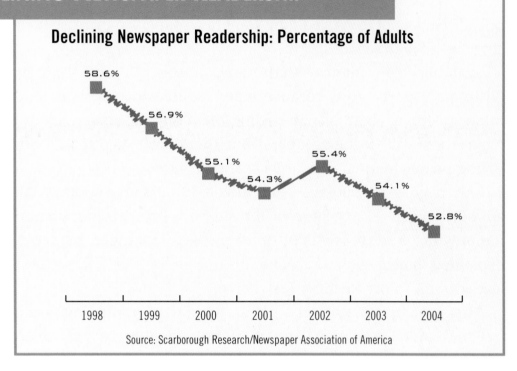

Declining Newspaper Readership: Percentage of Adults

58.6%

56.9%

55.1%

54.3%

55.4%

54.1%

52.8%

1998   1999   2000   2001   2002   2003   2004

Source: Scarborough Research/Newspaper Association of America

A 1991 poll by the Gallup Youth Survey found that "Teens are certainly interested in reading about the affairs of the world, but many would also like to see their daily newspaper present more information on what their fellow teens are thinking." The teens that Gallup surveyed offered suggestions on how to go about that. Eighty-five percent said they would like to read results of polls taken among fellow students and 84 percent said they would read general news about their local high schools.

Teen interest in music is ever-present, and the 1991 Gallup survey found that about three-fourths of the respondents were interested in reading music reviews by local teens. Coverage of celebrities that appeal to teens, such as pop singers and movie stars, has long been a staple of newspapers. Other stories that newspapers traditionally publish have a strong appeal to teenagers too, such as articles about high school sports. But teens seem to want even more: in the 1991 poll, 77 percent of teens said they want newspapers to increase their coverage of high school sports.

Another teen interest that many adults do not share is "extreme" sports. And because many adults do not share that interest, stories about skateboarding or mountain biking seldom make their way to newspapers. But there are exceptions. With young people in mind, the *Orlando Sentinel* last year began *Rush*, a weekly page in the sports section devoted to extreme sports. "We added the page . . . because of the subject's growing population nationwide, and because of its appeal to younger readers," explained Elaine Kramer, managing editor of the *Sentinel* and leader of its Young Readers Task Force.

However, a newspaper with a mission of providing local, national, and international news cannot possibly pay as much attention to teen interests as does MTV or a specialized magazine like *Rolling Stone*. Most of the news that newspapers have to cover do not directly involve teenagers. "Most news is about older people," writes Danny Schechter, a media analyst, in a study for Harvard University's Nieman Foundation for Journalism. "It's about people in power. Presidents and potentates. Corporations. Celebrities."

With this in mind, some newspapers are striving to give more prominence to stories about teenage life—stories that they hope interest teenagers as well as their parents. One example is a series on teenage pregnancy published by the *Orange County Register*. The newspaper's intention was not merely to write a story about teenagers, but to write it *for* teenagers.

The series began with reporter Bonnie Weston covering a routine news conference about pregnant and parenting teens. But Weston realized there was much more to the story than just dry statistics, so she convinced her editor to let her write an multi-part profile of the experiences of a particular 15-year-old mother and her boyfriend. Her editors advised her to write for a teenage audience, and she did. The articles focused on concrete details, such as stories by the parents' about how they chose the baby's name and their experiences during the first few weeks after bringing the baby home. They warned teenagers about the difficulties teen parents face, without lecturing to them.

The series won an award from the Casey Journalism Center on Children and Families. The newspaper received letters from teens about the series, and invited eight young people to join a panel to discuss the story.

But teen-oriented stories can sometimes raise controversy. Last year *Voices*, the weekly youth supplement of the *Reading Eagle* in Pennsylvania, published a photo of a group of teenagers, some of whom were making hand signs. Some adults contacted the newspaper to complain that the gestures were gang-related. "They weren't gang signs, but that didn't stop adults from calling and e-mailing," said editor Lisa Scheid. "I know these adults meant well in expressing their concern, but by jumping to conclusions they insulted those teenagers." The lesson, she added, is that when aiming at teenagers it is important to show reality even if it may be misunderstood by older people. "*Voices* has built its reputation on showing teens as they really are, now how someone wants them to be or thinks they should be."

Sharpening the Edge

Selecting the right kinds of stories — the kinds of "serious" stories teens want to read — is only part of the battle. When the Gannett newspaper chain created a "Gen-X Task Force" to figure out how to

attract younger readers, it found they were looking for a kind of writing that has never been part of the traditional journalistic style newspapers have been following for decades. "Why is your newspaper so boring?" one young reader asked. "You've got no style. You've got no edge. You certainly aren't much fun to read."

Gannett editors were taken aback by the force of the criticisms. But there was a lesson to be learned. To capture teen readers, it takes more than just publishing stories about music, high school sports, or teen life. What also matters is how those stories are written and laid out. "A black-and-white headline with a long story is not enough anymore," noted Task Force member Brad Robertson. "We need poignant photos, art, breakout boxes, charts, strong headlines, full color, Web links, cool ads, organization and attitude."

The 1990 study by Cathy J. Cobb-Walgren agreed with this assessment. It found that young people not only wished for more teen-oriented stories, but also that newspapers were more like magazines—smaller and in full color.

Over the last decade or so newspaper have not gotten smaller, but they certainly have taken up color. One of the first was *USA Today*, which broke new ground in 1982 with its colorful graphics and photographs. Today, nearly all medium- to large-circulation daily newspapers use color. But making a splash with color is not enough, editors say.

"[Young people] want like writing that has personality and voice," *Orlando Sentinel* managing editor Elaine Kramer believes. How to inject that into stories? After a study of what younger people wanted in the paper, staffers agreed the way to do it was with "narrative accounts and vivid stories told through the experiences of real people." Other newspapers staffers charged with attracting younger readers agree that teens think newspaper writing is too stodgy—and that it is time to shake up tradition.

"Instill in all reporters the need to consider different generations when reporting and writing, breaking down for young, old and in-between what the latest news means for them," Colleen Pohlig, editor of *Next*, the weekly youth section of the *Seattle Times*, told the Nieman Foundation. Younger readers, she believes, want stories that are "shorter but with substance and authority. This generation is all about quick-hit information gathering—not dumbed-down news, mind you, just shorter, smarter news stories."

Those shorter, more colorful youth-oriented stories often appear in special sections like *Next*. The *Seattle Times* is one of a growing number of newspapers across the nation that have some sort of youth content—ranging from a single weekly page to an entire separate supplement. Nevertheless, editors fear that if they take it too far, the writing will seem phony. Jane Marshall, editor of *Yo!*, the youth section of the *Houston Chronicle*, said her reporters do not try to pretend they are teenagers. "We don't try to be cool in the writing because we're never as cool as they are, and we don't use a lot of lingo because by the time we hear it, it's not even used anymore."

Of course, faking it is not a problem for youth sections that publish teen writers who bring a sensibility and point of view distinctly their own. The topics they cover are often unique to young people. For instance, one issue of *TeenScene*, of the central New Jersey *Home News Tribune*, featured a column from a teen girl about to buy her first car and a report about what Valentine's Day is like at a local high school—stories that an adult reporter could not possibly cover from the same vantage point.

"In the last year or two, some hardened reporters have seen what kids are writing and say, 'This [writing by teens] is profound,'" recalled Bob Welch, youth editor for the *Register-Guard* in Eugene, Oregon. "They're writing about what it's like when you walk into a cafeteria and two of your classmates get shot, giving up your kid for adoption, living with a boyfriend. And it's starting to wake up some of our readers and editors."

Working with inexperienced young writers, however, brings its own set of problems. Eric Elkins, editor of the *Colorado Kids* supplement to the *Denver Post*, explains, "Kids speak to other kids in a way that we can't." Yet at the same time his job as an editor is to correct basics such as grammar and sentence mechanics without losing the teen writers' youthful tone. Getting that tone in the newspaper is, after all, the reason editors publish stories written by teens.

To Jeffery Womble, editor of *Flipside* in the Fayetteville (N.C.) *Observer*, it is important to not discourage kids by simply rewriting their stories. "I explain what I'm changing and why, thus making it a partnership. I have to make the decision of whether to take this out or leave it in because they're speaking to their peers," he told the Newspaper Association of America.

Teenage reporters can even make contributions to the other sections of the newspaper, but they are sometimes ignored. Lorraine Eaton, past president of the Youth Editors Association of America, recalls that when she was editor of the *Teenology* section of the *Virginian-Pilot*, a front-page story about rising drug use among youth "contained quotes from experts, local adult leaders, and politicians, but not one teen-ager. This despite the fact that every reporter at our newspaper has a copy of the names and phone numbers of all of our 100 or so high school correspondents."

An omission like that is not just a failure in reaching out to teens. It is also a journalistic mistake in general, because a good news story about teenage drug use needs quotes from teenagers about drug use. Still, many newspapers are making the effort to attract young people, whether through dedicated pages or with livelier writing and more graphics in the main sections. What makes it more difficult is competition from other media—media teens seem to prefer anyway.

The Effect of Television

Young people's preference for shorter, more colorful stories comes from television. According to a 2003 Gallup Poll, only one in 100 American teens say they never watch television, and 11 percent said they watch more than 20 hours of television each week. All that heavy viewing has for at least a generation created "quick-hit" media habits. As a young woman said at a panel that the *Orlando Sentinel* set up to learn what young people thought about getting news from print as opposed to electronic media, "The newspaper is almost, like, outdated, because there are more entertaining ways to get the same information."

Why? For one thing, teens say, it is easier to sit back and watch television than to read a newspaper. For another, television moves much faster. A television news story, for instance, consists of quick moving images accompanied by script and interviews that are much shorter than traditional newspaper stories. One journalist famously noted years ago that all of the words heard in a network newscast can fit just on the front page of the *New York Times*.

But newspaper content cannot be tailored for television without huge expense. It would take huge investments in cameras, a studio, transmission equipment, and on-air talent. No newspaper has wanted to take that step, which is why there are no national newspapers that attempt to reproduce the entire print content of their daily publications on a television newscast.

Some editors believe that the way to compete with television is to be more like television. That's the philosophy at *USA Today*, which uses lots of color photographs and graphics, and runs news stories that are short in comparison to those in most other newspapers. A different approach is to build on the inherent strengths of newspapers by featuring stories that are more in-depth and longer in length.

Still, newspapers are not likely to disappear because of competition from television. Newspapers are portable, can be read anywhere, and readers do not need fancy technology to access their content. A newspaper can be stuck in a backpack to read in the cafeteria or between classes. The challenge for editors remains to get teens to put that paper in their backpacks.

Credibility is at the heart of trust between newspapers and their readers, the ultimate key that will determine whether a teen does put that paper in the backpack and, a few years later, in that brief-case on the way to the office. Credibility, however, has little to do with the print versus broadcast or online debate. No matter how many more teen-interest stories become part of regular coverage, no matter how edgy writing becomes, no matter how many special teen sections newspapers publish in print or online, newspapers will have to overcome negative perceptions teens have about them.

The problem has been getting worse over the years, not better, as both teens and adults are skeptical of the news media. In 1985 a Gallup poll showed that 55 percent of adults believed news organizations generally "get the facts straight," while 34 percent thought "reports are often inaccurate." By 2003, only 36 percent of adults believed news reports were accurate, with 62 percent saying they were not. That year, the Gallup Organization also found that 45 percent of adult respondents believed news reporting was slanted toward liberals, while 14 percent said the bias favored conservatives and 39 percent believed the news media was objective. Yet despite this distrust, some teens have a respect for newspapers that editors can build upon to develop a more trusting relationship.

Chapter Six

Magazines are able to focus on more specific audiences than newspapers. In recent years, magazines devoted to teen girls have become very popular.

Teen Magazines: The Wrong Message?

No matter how hard newspaper editors try to attract young readers, the basic newspaper will never focus exclusively on teens. Whether it's the *New York Times* or the Harlingen, Texas, *Valley Morning Star*, daily newspapers are by definition made for a broad readership. But it is a different story for magazines. They can specialize as much as they want—and a good number of them are aimed squarely at young people. There are magazines like *Young Rider*, for kids interested in horses, and *Game Informer*, for video gamers. A larger category is the "fanzines," aimed at girls up to their early teens and focused on gossip about popular musicians and movie or television stars with youth appeal. These include *J-14, Twist, BOP,* and the oldest of the type, *Tiger Beat*, which started in 1957 when Elvis Presley was a teen idol.

Another magazine with a focus on celebrities is *Teen People*, the third best-selling teenage magazine with an average annual circulation of about 1.6 million in 2004. It is different from the fanzines, because it also appeals to an older teenage audience and also has profiles of young people who are not famous, yet are doing something interesting. *Teen People's* editors get a lot of input from the magazine's "trendspotters," a network of 15,000 teenagers who help decide what articles are published, part of an effort to give teens what they want. The graphic look, too, is designed to visually attract teens. "It's very three-dimensional," *Teen People* editor Amy Barnett told *Media Life* magazine when the new look was inaugurated in 2003. "It has sort of a collage feel, as if the reader put it together herself."

A Fight for Survival?

But the decision of *Teen People* to empower its trendspotters and unveil a new teen-friendly design came about because of a slump in sales among teen magazines. Back in the late 1990s general interest teen magazines aimed at girls, such as *Seventeen* and *YM,* were among the hottest segments in magazine publishing. A Gallup Youth Survey at that time found that 53 percent of teens — including 58 percent of girls — said they had read a magazine the previous day. Although this figure was not as high as the 90 percent who watched television or the 89 percent who had listened to the radio the previous day, it nonetheless represented a large market for magazine publishers. In those years publications for teen girls seemed so profitable that publications aimed at adults began versions for teens: *People* launched *Teen People* in 1998 and *Cosmopolitan* followed with *Cosmo Girl* two years later. *Elle* joined in with *Elle Girl* in 2001 and *Vogue* with *Teen Vogue* in 2003.

However, at the same time the availability of other media — particularly the Internet — began to cut into the number of magazine readers. With such attractions as surfing the Web and sending instant messages to friends, there was less time for teenagers to read magazines. In 2002 *Teen*, the fourth-largest magazine for teenage girls, went out of business after a 23 percent downturn in circulation over the previous six months.

Aside from the celebrity-driven *Teen People* there are a number of general-interest monthly magazines marketed to teen girls. *Seventeen*, *YM*, and *Cosmo Girl* are all in the top 100 most widely sold magazines in the United States according to the Audit Bureau of Circulation (ABC), an independent group that monitors sales of newspapers and magazines. *Seventeen* is the largest, with a paid circulation of about 2.3 million in 2004, and also the oldest, founded in 1944. But *Seventeen* was among the worst-hit in the teen magazine slump of the early 2000s, losing more than 147,000 in average monthly circulation between 1997 and 2003. Some critics said the problem was that the magazine's identity was "muddled" because it tried to be all things to all teen girls. So in 2003 a new editor sharpened the focus to make it "a young woman's premier style and beauty magazine . . . tailored for women in their late teens and early twenties," as the magazine itself puts it. Executives say newsstand sales started going up in the first half of 2004.

YM is a magazine that battled *Seventeen* for largest circulation. Unlike its chief competitor, *YM* saw readership actually increase in the midst of the overall downturn—*YM* was up more than 260,000 in average circulation between 1997 and 2002. Yet between 2002 and 2003 circulation went down 3 percent, to about 2.2 million. Perhaps more important, income from advertisements decreased 41 percent year-to-year through February 2004. To fight the downward trend *YM* gave up its pink bubble-gum graphics to appeal to older teens, emphasizing fashion as well as young musicians and actors. This effort proved unsuccessful, and in the fall of 2004 *YM*'s publisher announced that it would stop producing the magazine after the January 2005 issue, and that its subscription list and assets would be sold.

Like the other magazines, *Cosmo Girl* covers beauty and fashion, but its claim to fame is articles and columns on relationships. "Not only does it have the best fashion and make-up tips, it has the best guy advice you could ask for," one reader named Emily said on Amazon.com. Perhaps because of that it has experienced steady growth in recent years. Between 2002 and 2003, circulation jumped 18.5 percent to about 1.26 million readers.

Two other magazines are, like *Cosmo Girl*, spinoffs of magazines for adult women. *Elle Girl* had a circulation of 405,374 in 2003, the first year it was audited. Aside from the standard emphasis on teen fashion and shopping, *Elle Girl* editors say the magazine tries to stand out by offering "Lots of [do it yourself] ideas, and other

ADVERTISING REVENUE OF TEEN MAGAZINES, 2003–2004

Magazine	2004	2003	+/-
Seventeen	$73,249,630	$89,383,066	-18%
Teen People	$49,401,852	$56,483,587	-12.5%
Cosmo Girl	$48,050,106	$41,412,493	+16%
YM	$44,316,392	$82,788,677	-46.5%
Teen Vogue	$25,142,845	$11,351,963	+121.5%
Elle Girl	$15,251,547	$9,862,299	+54.6%
Boys' Life	$3,818,489	$3,504,150	+9%
All magazines	$14,908,324,440	$13,588,643,744	+9.7%

Source: Magazine Publishers of America.

fun stuff for girls searching for a witty, smart alternative to the traditional teen magazine." *Teen Vogue* is the newest entry in the field, with a circulation estimated at about 325,000. The goal of *Teen Vogue* is to be a fashion authority, offering what its editors call a sophisticated focus on clothes and beauty while playing down traditional teen magazine fare such as relationship advice and celebrity coverage.

Hot to Look Hot

Some media experts are critical of the magazines aimed at teenage females, saying they place too much emphasis on good looks and popularity. "The magazines envision teen-age girls' lives as endless popularity contests," wrote Sheila Gibbons in an article about the subject. "School is the main stage for efforts to attain popularity and snag a boyfriend (you can't have one without the other, it seems), but mostly school is merely that—an environment for socializing. These magazines have little to say to girls about the value of academic achievement, civic engagement, or intellectual challenges."

Is Gibbons right? A look at the covers of several teen magazines shows they indeed emphasize looks and fashion. Typical cover teaser headlines include "256 Ways to Be a Beach Goddess" (*Elle Girl*, May 2004), "Look Hot! Swimsuits that Rule the Beach" (*YM*, June 2004), and "Trick to Flatten Your Belly" (*Seventeen*, August 2004). Inside, all the magazines are very similar, also—all are full of thin young women modeling skimpy clothes, attractive young men, and celebrities—fashionable female stars for readers to imitate, young studs for readers to fantasize about.

In a society where 36 percent of teen girls believe themselves overweight, according to a 2004 Gallup Poll, this idealization of the ultra-thin body can lead to unhealthy behavior among girls and young women. A 1999 study by the American Academy of Pediatrics found that 69 percent of girls surveyed admitted that magazine models influence their idea of the perfect body shape. Forty-seven percent of the girls tried to lose weight because of the pictures, even though only 29 percent of those surveyed were actually overweight.

Some experts have suggested that the desire to be like models shown in the popular media can cause some girls to develop eating disorders such as anorexia nervosa and bulimia. Magazines in particular have been singled out for blame. "Magazines, not television, seem to have the strongest relationship to eating disorders," says Rose M. Kundanis, author of *Children, Teens, Families, and Mass Media: The Millennial Generation*. "Researchers explain that because television encourages the consumption of high-fat foods, the effect toward eating disorders is minimized. On the other hand, magazines offer more instruction on dieting and therefore seem to be more significantly correlated to eating disorders."

Sex is another issue brought up by critics of magazines for teen girls. They note that all the photos of beautiful people and tips about beauty, fashion, and thinness have one underlying theme—catching a guy. "Magazines for teens blast girls with urgings to maximize their 'hot' looks while promoting the virginal ideal," wrote Sheila Gibbons. "Impressionable teens (and pre-teens) are being whipsawed by the mixed messages. Tips on how to look hot and sneak lip-locks with a beau at the school locker are interspersed with warnings to keep sexual matters from getting out of hand."

A story in the April 2004 issue of *Teen People*, for instance, warned against choosing to have sex at a young age. Yet in the same issue readers wrote in to tell about their first kiss ("My summer fling and I were hanging out in the back of some parking lot," one 16-year old reported) and a few pages later boys were asked what they thought about "girls who make the first move." (One young man responded, "It means she's really feeling me and ambitious enough to go after what she wants.") *Teen People* is not alone. In the fall of 2004 *Cosmo Girl* launched a "Battle of the Boys" contest in which girls were asked to send pictures of the "hottest guy" they know, with prizes for the winners as voted by readers. And *Seventeen* runs a regular feature called "Guy Talk," in which teen boys give advice ranging from the best pickup lines to summer date ideas.

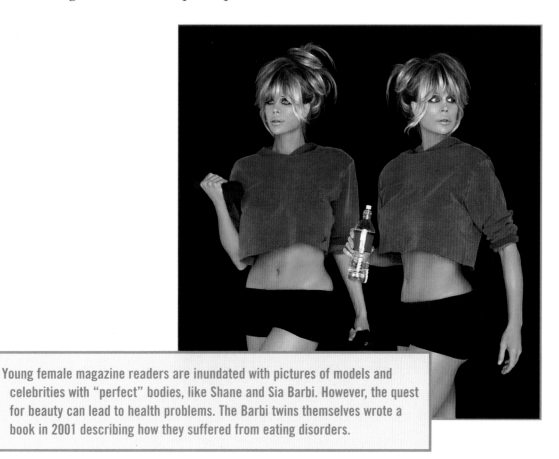

Young female magazine readers are inundated with pictures of models and celebrities with "perfect" bodies, like Shane and Sia Barbi. However, the quest for beauty can lead to health problems. The Barbi twins themselves wrote a book in 2001 describing how they suffered from eating disorders.

Editors defend their publications, arguing that there is nothing wrong with stories about guys and dating. Besides, they insist, their magazines have to offer celebrity coverage, guy advice, and beauty and fashion tips because that is what teen girls want to read. Editors can also point to coverage of more serious issues. Along with the parade of beautiful models and fashion advice in the summer 2004 issue of *Teen Vogue*, there was a story on the growing problem of young girls who are so depressed they cut their bodies "to turn their ulterior emotional pain into something undeniably physical." In May 2004 *Elle Girl* included an article about how the AIDS epidemic in Africa affects teen girls on that continent. *Seventeen* regularly runs articles on college that focus not only on campus social life but also academics. And with regard to the worship of thin celebrity bodies, *YM* ran a story in June 2004 that advises readers to "realize that many of the pictures in magazines are retouched." The article went on, "It's true a lot of celebrities are ridiculously, unhealthily skinny. But there are a precious handful of women who manage to be famous *and* eat once in a while." With the text *YM* included photos of celebrities not particularly famous for being skinny, like actress Drew Barrymore and soccer player Mia Hamm.

Magazines for Boys

In general, fewer boys than girls regularly read magazines. The top 100 magazines, according to circulation figures audited by the ABC, includes *Game Informer* (number 63), whose readership probably includes a large percentage of teen boys. Outside the top 100 publications there are several other magazines, like *Daily Bread Inline Skate Magazine* or the rock music-oriented *Spin,* which also attract a fair share of male teenagers. But there is just one general-interest magazines for boys that is as widely read as *Seventeen*, *YM*, and other publications for girls — *Boys' Life*, with a circulation of about 1.3 million.

Yet *Boys' Life* is different from other general circulation magazines one might come across at a store. It has been published by the Boy Scouts of America since 1911 (the Girl Scouts also have their own publication, *Girls' Life*) and its circulation relies heavily on the Scouts' membership. Many of the articles in *Boys' Life* cover activities related to Boy Scouts, like camping. So in a sense, there is no general interest magazine in the United States for teen boys. Instead, a study by Horizon Media concluded, "Male teens are more likely to read comic books and wrestling and video game publications."

Why don't magazines appeal to teenage boys the way that they do to teen girls? "I don't think teen boys want to be told what to do, how to act, or how to dress," explained media executive J. Eric Bethel in an article published by *American Demographics* in 2000. Another media analyst, Fran Richards, added, "the traditional female model of service-only magazines won't work for boys."

So far, Richards appears to be right. In the early 1990s, a magazine called *Dirt* offered information about music, sports, gadgets, fashion, and dating tips. It quickly failed. In 2000, the adult men's magazine *Men's Health* launched a spinoff for teen boys called *MH-18*. Its excited editors told *American Demographics* their magazine was going to show male teens how to "get strong, be smart, look good, have fun . . . and get the girl." But they found that male teens did not want that kind of advice, at least not from a magazine. *MH-18* shut down the year after it started. It will probably be a while before somebody tries again.

Chapter Seven

TiVo Central

Now Playing on TiVo
Watch Live TV
Music & Photos
Showcases & TV Guide®
Pick Programs to Record
TiVo Messages & Setup

SONY

Examples of media convergence include devices like TiVo, which combines television and movies with computers.

The Future Converges

In the mid- to late-1980s, the Gallup Organization did a series of surveys on young people and computers. "The number of teens studying computers is at an all-time high," one Gallup survey found in 1989. (At the time, the figure was 36 percent—very low by today's standards.) Back then, "computers" was a school subject, something to be studied, perhaps for a future career. Today, it is much more than that. With the popularity of the Internet, teens are spending a lot more of their free time with computers. By 2003 the Gallup Youth Survey was finding that, for example, 96 percent of teenagers who spend at least five hours online per week said they use the Internet for finding information. Before the Internet, of course, looking up information was mostly done through printed media such as newspapers or books found in libraries.

It is a reminder that the Web is so widespread in the United States it has become a part of the mass media, like television, radio, newspapers, and magazines. But there is more to it. The Internet is not merely one more medium. It has the potential to replace all other forms of mass media—without really replacing them, in a way.

This is due to the very nature of the Internet, which can do much that other media cannot. Print media includes text and photographs or illustrations, but not sound or moving pictures. Radio has sound, but no text or visuals. Television has sound, video and, theoretically, it can also display text—but nobody is likely to sit in front of a television set reading a long article like they would with a newspaper.

The Internet is the only medium that can deliver all of these elements: still pictures and graphics, video, and text. Plus, it offers interactivity unmatched by any other media. Because of the Internet's versatility, many experts predict the wave of the future is media *convergence*—in years to come, they say, all mass media will come through the computer. To teens today who grew up using the Internet, this might seem the normal road to follow.

To some mass media executives, convergence is a good thing. After all, people online will still be able to read long news articles or even books, and watch television programs or listen to music. It's just that they will do it in a different place instead of the traditional physical newspaper or the old-fashioned television and radio sets.

Other executives worry about the future. For instance, while radio's transition to the Internet is relatively easy technically and editorially (it is not difficult to send audio online to home computers, and there is no need to change content), measuring ratings can be a problem. Already many radio programs are available live on the Web, but companies such as Arbitron have not begun to count the online audience—ratings are still based on listeners on traditional radio sets. So the more people who switch to the Internet to listen to their favorite show, the more the radio station's ratings decrease.

At some point, the radio industry will probably find a reliable way to count its Internet audience. For television, however, convergence is more complicated. TV executives and producers are not sure how to make the transition from programs distributed via cable or satellite to programs distributed exclusively online.

Several companies are already working on this issue. TiVo, known for its digital video system that allows users to pre-set recordings of television shows whether transmitted on cable, satellite, or the airwaves, announced in June 2004 plans for a new service that also lets users download movies and music from the Internet for playback on TiVo's recorders. "It is just one of a growing group of large and small companies that are looking at high-speed Internet to deliver video content to the living room," reported the *New York Times*. Other video distributors, including the Blockbuster chain of stores, are also exploring ways to deliver movies via the Internet. Users could download the movies and view them later.

To be sure, sending music or even movies over the Internet for downloading is different from making television programs available online at the same time they are transmitted the old-fashioned way. That is not happening much yet. "Streaming" shows online for immediate viewing, with the same high quality video of cable, satellite, or a strong over-the-air signal, can only work with broadband connections faster than most people have. Yet the number of people using high-speed internet connections is growing, which has led Microsoft and other companies to believe it will eventually be possible to deliver programming on the Internet with the video quality viewers are used to on their television sets. They have started working on technology to do exactly that. Cable companies, too, are not standing still. As Steve Burke, president of Comcast Cable, the largest cable operator in the U.S. told the *New York Times* when TiVo announced its Internet recording service, "We're big believers that the Internet is the future."

While television-Internet convergence remains in the future, newspapers face convergence *now*. Video needs broadband, but text and most graphics do not. As a result, newspapers have jumped on the Internet.

Just about every major newspaper in the world already has an Internet edition. Editors find it relatively inexpensive to run a website because they use stories already written for the print edition. These are supplemented by additional graphic features and interactive innovations that are only possible online, such as chats with reporters, columnists, or editors. Editors seeking teen readers are also happy that a newspaper's Web-based content gives young people the flash and color that they want.

The Internet has inherent advantages over print. When teenagers want to find something about a particular subject—a favorite band, for instance, or the latest news on skateboarding—they can go to a search engine like Google, enter a few key words, hit enter, and get hundreds if not thousands of Web pages with the information they seek. Print offers nothing remotely as easy. As the *Washington Post's* Steve Coll said to the Nieman Foundation, "search technology is altering in profound ways [young people's] relationship with information and media."

As a result, editors are concerned that web-based "newspapers" might in the future become so popular they drive print editions out of business. They worry that even the web-based versions of their own newspapers might turn out to be the enemy. All those Web readers force newspapers into a balancing act—how to make Internet editions complement, not replace, the traditional newspaper?

Like other editors, Coll knows that changing media habits caused by the Internet are a reality that is not about to go away, and that newspapers must deal with. However he and an increasing number of editors believe that "dealing with it" means seeing the Web not only as competition, but also as an opportunity. "[Younger people] are going to have a less deep and less loyal relationship

Microsoft chairman Bill gates holds a tablet PC has he speaks about newspapers and technology at the annual Newspaper Association of America convention in Seattle. Gates said that advances in technology such as better note-taking software and online newspaper design programs could help papers evolve and attract new readership.

with newspapers. But they're going to have some relationship," he said. The goal, Coll believes, is for newspapers to retain the loyalty of today's young people by presenting their product—news and advertising—online as well as in print. "At the *Washington Post*, the total audience across all platforms that consumes our journalism has roughly quintupled in four years. That accounts for an enormous new Web audience we've attracted."

The question, Coll and other journalists acknowledge, is not whether to go online, but how much to offer online—how to design and fill a website that attracts the younger generation without damaging the printed edition. "You have to continue to operate in ways that serve the next day's newspaper without yielding an inch. But in doing so you have to change to deliver simultaneously to this new and crucially important new medium," Coll said.

Nobody knows how to do that, exactly. Some editors prefer to limit their newspaper's online content. The Website of *Red Eye*, the supplement for young readers published in the *Chicago Tribune*, intentionally omits most of the articles that appear in the print edition. "If we . . . put all our content online, how would that help us build a daily newspaper habit?" said Joe Knowles, *Red Eye's* editor. "We chose to make the site a 'teaser,' with just a reproduction of the day's cover and just a few stories."

Other experts disagree. Journalism professor John Hartman believes daily newspapers should add a free weekly print supplement aimed at young readers and make its entire content (as well as the "regular" content of the daily newspaper) available online, for free. "Newspapers can use the weekly readership and Web site visits to sell the merits of the daily print publication," he wrote. "Some young people might grow into users of the Web, the weekly, and the daily. If not, two out of three ain't bad."

Other journalists go further. They have come to believe the physical newspaper may disappear. "Maybe we shouldn't care so much about paper. Is our real concern whether magazines and newspapers disappear, or is it that we want kids to read?" Thomasz Souto Correa, former editor of Latin America's largest magazine publisher, wrote in a Nieman Foundation report. "Does it matter if they read from a paper page or on a screen?"

The physical newspaper is likely to survive the Internet, even if only because it is easier to handle. A reader can hold it, fold it, and eventually throw it away. Souto Correa believes that when today's teens grow to adulthood they will continue to read books, newspapers, and magazines printed on paper, but as a complement to electronic media. "The difference is that today we complement the print media with the electronic media," he said. "This generation will do the opposite. Credible publications have to engage young readers both in print and on the Web."

Greater Focus on Teens

Teens of the future will be just as likely as teens of the past and present to be interested in, well, things that matter to teens. So they will continue to seek out that kind of information in the mass media, convergence or not. Because of that, and because of the increasing buying power of American young people, the media will continue to seek out teens.

That will happen in different degrees. The Big Three broadcast television networks are unlikely to become "teen" networks, leaving the market to smaller operations like WB, which are likely to continue their dependence on young people. Cable, of course, will always have the ability to target young people in different channels, as will radio.

In the future, computers and cellular phones will spread more of the world's information digitally.

Newspapers will continue to be mainly for adults, but some will probably have more youth-oriented pages. There will continue to be magazines for teenage girls—even if a couple of them go out of business—and maybe one day a smart editor might even figure out how to capture a *male* teen readership.

Some, or most, or even all of that teen content on the mass media will eventually work its way to the online world that teens are so comfortable handling. Nobody knows when, or to what extent, or exactly how it will all work. What is for certain is that teens will continue to live immersed in the sights and sounds produced by the mass media, and that the mass media—whatever that turns out to be—will continue to be influenced by the youth culture it helped create.

Glossary

Blog—short for 'Web log," a website where the owner maintains a regularly updated dairy about any subject, often his or her personal life.

Broadband—a fast Internet connection, usually through cable.

Broadcast networks—a television operation under a single programmer that uses the airwaves, as opposed to wire cables, for transmission. They are more regulated by the government than their counterparts on cable.

Browser—a computer program used to access the World Wide Web.

Cable networks—television stations under a single programmer that use cable, as opposed to the airwaves, for transmission.

Conglomerate—a group of diverse companies under one main corporation.

Convergence—the coming together of various elements, specially various media.

Demographic—a segment of a population broken down by characteristics such by age, income, race, etc.

Dial-up—a connection to the Internet that uses telephone lines; slower than broadband.

FTP—File Transfer Protocol, a method for sending or receiving digital files on the Internet.

Graphic interface—any computer program that executes commands by clicking on icons with a mouse, instead of typing instructions in a computer language.

Hyperlink—a reference on a Web page that takes the user to a different Internet location, usually by clicking on it.

Lead—in journalism, the most important story of the day, or of the first paragraph in any story.

Glossary

NEWSWORTHY—in journalism, a story interesting enough to warrant coverage.

RATING—the percentage of all households with television, including households where the set is turned off, that are tuned in to a particular program. A similar measurement, *share,* is the percentage of all households with the set *on* that are tuned in to a particular program.

SWEEPS—a one-month period during which the ratings of television stations are used to establish how much they will charge for advertisements. Usually held in February, May, and November.

TELNET—an Internet system that allows remote log-ins to individual computers.

UPLOAD—to send a file from a computer to the Internet, as opposed to download, which is to bring a file from the Internet to a computer.

Internet Resources

http://www.gallup.com

Visitors to the site maintained by The Gallup Organization can find results of Gallup Youth Surveys as well as many other research projects undertaken by the national polling firm.

http://teenblogs.studentcenter.org

A teen guide to creating blogs, with links to teenage bloggers. Included is a host of information on how teens can design, edit, organize, and maintain their individual blogs.

www.kff.org

The Henry J. Kaiser Family Foundation is a non-profit, private operating foundation that focuses on major healthcare issues. They develop and run their own research and communications programs, and have conducted studies about teens and the media.

www.medialifemagazine.com

Media Life is an online daily (Monday through Friday) newspaper that is written for media planners and buyers. Its mission is to tell the stories behind the headlines.

www.naa.org

The Newspaper Association of America (NAA) is a nonprofit organization that represents the newspaper industry. The Association focuses on six key strategic priorities: marketing, public policy, diversity, industry development, newspaper operations, and readership. Their website is an exhaustive source for information about the newspaper industry.

Internet Resources

www.pewinternet.org

The Pew Internet & American Life Project is a non-profit research center that studies the social effects of the Internet on families, communities, work and home, daily life, education, health care, civic and political life. The site has conducted studies about online teens and the impact of the Internet on their lives.

www.riaa.com

The website for the Recording Industry Association of America outlines the group's views about downloaded music. The organization defines music piracy, explains the penalties for copyright infringement, and provides information on how the RIAA enforces its members' copyrights.

www.tvtome.com

TV Tome provides guides and reviews for almost all the current shows on television, including many classics. In addition to episode guides, TV Tome provides information about over 250,000 people associated with TV—actors, writers, directors, and producers.

Further Reading

Buckingham, David. *After the Death of Childhood: Growing Up in the Age of Electronic Media*. Cambridge: Polity Press, 2000.

Douglas, Susan. *Where the Girls Are: Growing Up Female with the Mass Media*. New York: Three Rivers Press, 1995.

Dudley, William, ed. *Media Violence: Opposing Viewpoints*. San Diego: Greenhaven Press, 1999.

Fisherkeller, Joellen. *Growing Up With Television: Everyday Learning Among Young Adolescents*. Philadelphia: Temple University Press, 2002.

Kundanis, Rose M. Children, *Teens, Families, and Mass Media: The Millennial Generation*. Mahwah, N.J.: Lea, 2003

Rothman, Kevin. *Coping With Dangers on the Internet: A Teen's Guide to Staying Safe Online*. New York: Rosen Publishing Group, 2000.

Winn, Marie. *The Plug-In Drug: Television, Computers, and Family Life*. New York: Penguin USA, 2002.

Index

Numbers in **bold italic** refer to captions and graphs.

Index

Index

Index

Picture Credits

Contributors

GEORGE GALLUP JR. is chairman of The George H. Gallup International Institute (sponsored by The Gallup International Research and Education Center, or GIREC) and is a senior scientist and member of the GIREC council. Mr. Gallup serves on many boards in the area of health, education, and religion.

Mr. Gallup is recognized internationally for his research and study on youth, health, religion, and urban problems. He has written numerous books including *My Kids On Drugs?* with Art Linkletter (Standard, 1981), *The Great American Success Story* with Alec Gallup and William Proctor (Dow Jones-Irwin, 1986), *Growing Up Scared in America* with Wendy Plump (Morehouse, 1995), *Surveying the Religious Landscape: Trends in U.S. Beliefs* with D. Michael Lindsay (Morehouse, 1999), and *The Next American Spirituality* with Timothy Jones (Chariot Victor Publishing, 1999).

Mr. Gallup received his BA degree from the Princeton University Department of Religion in 1954, and holds seven honorary degrees. He has received many awards, including the Charles E. Wilson Award in 1994, the Judge Issacs Lifetime Achievement Award in 1996, and the Bethune-DuBois Institute Award in 2000. Mr. Gallup lives near Princeton, New Jersey, with his wife, Kingsley. They have three grown children.

THE GALLUP YOUTH SURVEY was founded in 1977 by Dr. George Gallup to provide ongoing information on the opinions, beliefs and activities of America's high school students and to help society meet its responsibility to youth. The topics examined by the Gallup Youth Survey have covered a wide range—from abortion to zoology. From its founding through the year 2001, the Gallup Youth Survey sent more than 1,200 weekly reports to the Associated Press, to be distributed to newspapers around the nation. Since January 2002, Gallup Youth Survey reports have been made available on a weekly basis through the Gallup Tuesday Briefing.

ROGER E. HERNÁNDEZ is a nationally syndicated columnist and the author of *Cubans in America* (Kensington Publishing, 2002) as well as several books for Mason Crest Publishers. He teaches journalism and English composition at the New Jersey Institute of Technology in Newark, where is writer-in-residence, and at Rutgers University. He lives with his family in New Jersey.